MORE OBITER DICTA

MORE
OBITER DICTA

BY

AUGUSTINE BIRRELL.

Essay Index Reprint Series

BOOKS FOR LIBRARIES PRESS
FREEPORT, NEW YORK

First Published 1924

Reprinted 1969

LIBRARY OF CONGRESS CATALOG CARD NUMBER:

68-57304

PRINTED IN THE UNITED STATES OF AMERICA

PREFACE

IT is always rash to make promises in print, and I do not, therefore, promise that this small volume will be my last collection of previously printed papers.

Yet probably it will be, since an author should be the first to cry, " Hold ! Enough."

This habit of clapping within the covers of a book, contributions, extending over years, to the periodical Press, which can hardly help being exposed to the charge of inherent insignificance, is a habit that should be kept in check ; yet, so ineradicable is a scribbler's vanity that, even at this moment of stern self-examination, I cannot quite bring myself to believe that even yet no single one of my still uncollected essays is worth republication in an accessible form. But I am beginning to believe it.

This, however, is clear to me as I sit handling the earliest copy of this little book, that, so long as I live, there will be one reader to whom it can never fail to give pleasure, not because of its merits—for the reader I have in mind is nothing if not critical, and knows those merits to be of the slightest—but on account of the pleasant memories that cluster round most of the years during which its contents were produced.

As this one reader is myself, I see no reason why I should not dedicate these " More Obiter Dicta " to him, and seize the opportunity, hitherto denied me, of telling him that his writings—" mere writings," to use the famous phrase of the editors of the First Folio of Shakespeare—would have been much better had he taken more pains.

Some changes have been made in the papers, but none of such a character as alters their original drift. The dates of their composition have been given, and in some cases their original domiciles.

I have to thank the Editors of *The Times* and of the *Nation* and *Athenæum* for permitting the republication of a few of the pieces included in this volume.

A. B.

CONTENTS

I.

ANTI-HUMBUG.

(1904.)

IT has been said by some one that to be a great judge a man must be a great brute—meaning intellectually a brute, and without implying any aspersion upon his humanity. If this saying had any meaning at all, it probably was intended to signify that the great current of law, as it comes down the generations, admits of no deviations, but must be allowed to flow in one deep channel, otherwise, what between floods and shallows, it will fritter itself away. Too refined a mind on the judicial bench has often proved very costly to the suitor.

And it is much the same with literary criticism, although bad criticism, unlike bad law, does not hit anybody, worth mentioning, in the pocket.

On the other hand, both judges and critics should beware of the other extreme, and be careful to avoid the affectation of brutality. Overrefinement is a snare, but a carefully cultivated coarseness of fibre is an abomination.

It is not easy to walk warily between these two ditches.

I have lately been re-reading the volumes named below,* containing the literary criticisms of Sir Leslie Stephen. His music, though not as sweet as is Apollo's lute, still sounds pleasantly on my ear, for it has a manly strain.

Had Sir Leslie Stephen lived in the eighteenth century—and in one of these volumes he states the terms on which he willingly would have done so—his essays might have been written above the signature "Anti-humbug." In fact, his single shortcoming as a philosopher and critic is the dominance he has allowed to this one note. If too much insisted upon, the hearer grows restive, the attitude of mind becomes a little irksome. Perhaps, for all we know—so we murmur to ourselves—a sunrise in the Alps is all humbug, but it is very beautiful. The cure for this, however, is simple enough : it is to lay this critic down for a while, and to read the books of other people ; after a bit you will need another dose of anti-humbug.

There is no use trying to delude Sir Leslie

* "Hours in a Library," 3 vols. ; "Studies of a Biographer," 4 vols.

Stephen ; he simply will not be cheated—not even by himself. Take the case of the " Dictionary of National Biography," a huge undertaking started under his editorship, and to which he has made numerous lengthy, though highly condensed, contributions. He is proud of the Dictionary ; he keeps recurring to it ; he turns over its volumes with a paternal pride ; but when his successor, Sir Sidney Lee, at the Royal Institution, indulges himself in a small delusion about " the commemorative instinct " being the basis on which the sixty volumes are built, the old watchdog begins to bark—he has scented humbug.

When the old " Biographia Britannica " was coming out Cowper made the unpleasant remark that it was

> " A fond attempt to give a deathless lot
> To names ignoble, born to be forgot."

If that was a fair judgment, what are we to say to the modern work, which includes thousands of names too obscure for mention in its predecessor ? When Mr. Lee speaks of " the commemorative instinct " as justifying his undertaking, the enemy replies that a very small minority of the names deserve commemoration. To appeal to instinct is to repudiate reason and to justify monomania. Admitting, as we all admit, the importance of keeping alive the leading names of history, what is the use of this long procession of the hopelessly insignificant ? Why repeat the familiar formula about the man who was born on such a day, was " educated at the grammar school of his native town," became a fellow of his college, took a living, married, published a volume of poems which nobody has read for a century or two, and has been during all that time in his churchyard ? Can he not be left in peace ? Is it not almost a mockery to persist in keeping up some faint and flickering image of him above ground ? . . . Why struggle against the inevitable ? Better oblivion than a permanent admission that you were thoroughly and hopelessly commonplace. I confess that I sometimes thought as much when I was toiling in my old treadmill, now Mr. Lee's. Much of the work to be done was uninteresting if not absolutely repulsive.

This is excellent good sense, but in a dictionary-maker unexpected. To jeer at your own hobby-horse, and to point out that in sober truth he is a spavined brute, is a morality almost too bracing. Stephen's favourite wind is due east. And yet why should we wish to be deceived ? Sir Leslie Stephen makes out an excellent case for the Dictionary, without pretending that it does more than seek to gratify an intelligent curiosity, to fill the gaps of history, and to tell the student where to find the authorities he must consult before he publishes his brochure. " It should be," says the editor, " a confidential friend, constantly at their elbow—giving them a summary of the knowledge of antiquaries, genealogists, bibliographers, as well as historians, upon every collateral point which may happen for the moment to be relevant. But," Sir Leslie feels impelled to add, " it must be admitted that it is bound to be rather dry."

What is a little curious is that this biographer is obviously very fond of detail. In these volumes he tells the story of Scott's ruin as if he were an accountant ; nor did the troublesome details of Pope's epistolary frauds ever seem to tease him. But, willing as he is to ride his hobby, the one thing he will not submit to, is to be told that his Pegasus is of celestial origin. Of Johnson, Gibbon, Arthur Young, and Wordsworth he writes with fullness of knowledge and sureness of touch ; and if one turns from them to the names of Arnold, Jowett, and Tennyson, it is not because old things are not still the best, but because one likes to see a critic with whose methods we are already familiar get to work upon fresh matter. We know how Sir Leslie Stephen regards the eighteenth century ; let us watch him handle the nineteenth. As we expected, it makes no difference. The sky is changed, but not the disposition. The lecture on Matthew Arnold is most attractive and engaging. What can be pleasanter than this ?

The reasons against my enterprise are indeed so strong that I am now almost ashamed to mention them. In the first place, I knew Arnold personally, though I cannot boast of having known him so intimately as to be provided with reminiscences. At one of my meetings with him, indeed, I do remember a remark which was made which struck me at the moment as singularly happy. Unfortunately, it was a remark made by me, and not by him. Nothing, therefore, should induce me to report it, though, if you attend to what I am about to say, you will perhaps hear it and, I hope, recognise it by this description. But though our acquaintance was not so close as I could have wished, it left me with a singularly strong impression of Arnold's personal charm. Though some objects of my worship were to him mere wooden idols ; though I once satisfactorily confuted him in an article, now happily forgotten by myself and everybody else ; though I was once even his editor, and forced in that capacity to decline certain articles—on grounds, of course, quite apart from literary merit—yet he was always not only courteous, but cordial, and I may almost say affectionate, in manner.

This is most agreeable writing. Stephen, we rejoice to notice, holds the true faith about Arnold :

Whatever else he was, Arnold was a genuine poet. I believe in poetry which learns itself by heart. So " Sohrab and Rustum " is to me among the most delightful of modern poems. I can always read " Tristram and Iseult " and the " Church of Brou," and " Empedocles on Etna." I have never got out of my head, since I read it, the little poem about the Neckan who sings his plaintive song on the Baltic headlands, or the verses about the dachshund Geist, whose grave at Cobham should be a goal for all poetic pilgrims.

It is perhaps sad, but it is certainly true, that the most moving passages in the writings of critics are not those in which they expound their principles, but just those in which, in the simple language of the heart, they avow their preferences or confess their abhorrence of particular books, poems, and pictures.

For one vein of Arnold's poetic thought Sir Leslie Stephen has no liking—he sees humbug in it : the melancholy vein that deplores the with-

drawing tide of belief and talks of anodynes. " I
fail," he says, " to appreciate these musical moans
over spilt milk." But Arnold never shed a tear
over spilt milk himself; what he was able to do
was to comprehend, both dramatically and intellectually, those who did, and to give utterance to
their sorrow. A poet does not know his business
if he cannot make fiddle-strings out of other
people's feelings. Arnold's religious opinions
puzzle Stephen's practical mind. Dogmas may
not be true, but they do bind. " Could St. Paul,"
it is asked, " have spread the Church of the
Gentiles without the help of the theories which
Arnold regarded as accretions ? " Mr. Arnold
would, we feel sure, have answered " No ! but
what then ? " " Would the beautiful spirit of the
mystics have conquered the world as well as
touched the hearts of a few hermits without the
rigid framework of dogmas in which they were
set ? " Perhaps not ; but the useful presence of
alloy does not either disprove nor disparage the
pure metal, which may ultimately be strong
enough to stand alone.

Mr. Jowett is a fine subject for Sir Leslie
Stephen. " What was the secret and the real
nature of Jowett's remarkable influence ? "

Stephen apologises for not belonging to the University of Oxford, and consequently for regarding with the eyes of an outsider that " singular and slightly absurd phenomenon called the Oxford Movement." But the conclusion at which he arrives is that the intellectual enterprise on which Jowett was engaged was

a hopeless endeavour to hide irreconcilable contrasts and pretend that they did not exist, and was injurious to the higher interests of intellectual honesty. He catches aspects of opinions and expresses them pithily, but he never can concentrate his mind or bring his doctrine to a focus ; the writing becomes discontinuous ; he wanders round and round problems without distinctly answering them or bringing the whole to an issue. He plays with philosophical principles without ever exactly saying Yes or No.

Well, even if he did, he had never need to play alone. " He stood at the parting of many ways, and he wrote ' No thoroughfare ' upon them all." What else could he write ? Most men are Jowetts without any Balliols to brag of. They do not believe in the actual occurrence of the supernatural facts on which Christianity is alleged to be based, but they are not prepared to take Sir Leslie's advice and drop them, because, firstly, they do not actively dislike them, and, secondly, they foresee great practical difficulties in getting on without them. Why should they sell out of a still going and dividend-paying concern when they have not the faintest idea where to look for another investment for their money ? Where was Jowett to go to if he gave up Balliol ? He was not a man of genius like Carlyle ; he could not write like Renan ; he had no enthusiasm for humanity ; he would not have been happy doing Archbishops of Canterbury for the "Dictionary of National Biography." So he stayed where he was, and Balliol got new buildings and a new cricket ground, and turned out quite a number of excellent young fellows warranted to come and go anywhere except to the gallows or the stake.

The only fault I can find with Sir Leslie Stephen as a critic is that he is so frightened of talking nonsense that he never reaches the altitudes where " the springs of knowledge are."

What he says of Charles Kingsley is, though for very different reasons, true of himself : " He is not at ease on those heights from which alone the widest truths become perceptible, and excite the emotions which are at once deepest and calmest." And yet this timidity of expressing emotion does not save Sir Leslie Stephen from occasionally talking nonsense. What critic with his range of reading can ever hope to do so ?

II.

SAMUEL TAYLOR COLERIDGE.

(1891.)

AIRS and floating echoes occasionally reach us syllabling the intelligence that, at last, after nearly sixty years of waiting, an authoritative Life of Samuel Taylor Coleridge ("beneficially abridged Esteesee") may be shortly expected. Whether rumour lies, as her wont is, we have not the slightest notion; and whilst unprepared to say that the airs and floating echoes before referred to are of the kind which, in the words of a poet who was very easily bored, "convey a melancholy into all our day," still neither can we truthfully assert that a really thick Life of Coleridge would be likely to make men merry. It is very easy to please some people, no doubt. It is narrated of Mr. Justice Wightman that he was once discovered out of term one very cold day gloating over a large fire and the "Life and Letters of Mrs. Hannah More." But old-fashioned judges

10

—and Wightman was that kind—were so much in the habit of listening to what was said to them in court, that they found it always gratifying to read to themselves when out of it.

It is odd to contrast the dignified place which Coleridge occupied at the time of his death, and still occupies in the minds of all lovers of literature, with the undignified creatures who wrote about him. Cottle, Gillman, Allsop are not names to conjure with. The unfortunate subject of their lucubrations seems never, whilst in their hands, to escape from a dull back-parlour in a third-rate street in a provincial town, with horsehair chairs and a stale smell of opium.

Joseph Cottle, the brother of Amos, the author of " The Sparrow and the Gudgeon " and an epic or two, is the best of these Coleridgian biographers, and his two volumes of " Early Recollections " contain many good things, oddly told ; but the general effect produced is shabby and unsatis-factory. A scholar, a poet with the finest ear in Europe, a critic like unto none before or since, ought not to be found writing dull, twaddling letters, even to Joseph Cottle. It may be attributable to lack of humour ; most things are nowadays. But Coleridge had humour, and sar·

casm too. He could ridicule, not only his friends,
but himself. Perhaps he did the former a little
more like life. He writes to Cottle :

> I sent to the *Monthly Magazine* (1797) three mock sonnets, in
> ridicule of my own poems and Charles Lloyd's and Lamb's,
> exposing that affectation of unaffectedness, of jumping and
> misplaced accent, in commonplace epithets, flat lines forced
> into poetry by italics (signifying how well and mouthishly the
> author would read them), puny pathos, etc., etc. The instances
> were almost all taken from myself and Lamb and Lloyd. I
> signed them Nehemiah Higginbotham. I think they may do
> good to our young bards. God love you.—S. T. C.

Here is one of the sonnets, " To Simplicity " ; it
is after Lamb :

> O ! I do love thee, meek Simplicity !
> For of thy lays the lulling simpleness
> Goes to my heart and soothes each small distress—
> Distress though small, yet haply great to me.
> 'Tis true on Lady Fortune's gentlest pad
> I amble on—yet though I know not why,
> So sad I am ! but should a friend and I
> Grow cold and miff, O ! I am very sad !
> And then with sonnets and with sympathy
> My dreamy bosom's mystic woes I pall,
> Now of my false friend 'plaining plaintively,
> Now raving at mankind in general ;
> But whether sad or fierce, 'tis simple all—
> All very simple—meek Simplicity.

Charles Lamb did not at all appreciate his poetical
partner and co-author turning the productions of
the firm into ridicule—but the sonnet " To Simplicity " may have done him good, as Coleridge
piously hoped, for all that.

Allsop must have been a figure of fun. His two volumes about Coleridge contain some interesting letters, lively criticism of Sir Walter Scott, and scraps of conversation ; but the ridiculous character of the compiler hangs over the whole book, and makes it almost contemptible. The story of the man with Lamb's smile is growing stale, but it can never altogether lose its charm. Here is it, italics and all :

I have said that I never knew any one who at all approached or resembled our delightful housemate. I am wrong. I once met a man with his smile. His smile. There is nothing like it upon earth, unless perchance this man survives. And yet how unlike in every other regard, personal and mental; not that the man who had by some most extraordinary means acquired or appropriated this *sunshine of the face* was at all deficient in mental qualities . . . He was, I believe, a stockbroker. . . . Yet this man had never known Lamb, still his smile was the same—the *selfsame* expression on a different face—if indeed whilst that smile passed it you could see any difference. To those who wish to see the only thing left on earth, *if it is still left*, of Lamb, his best and most beautiful remain, his smile, I will indicate its possessor—Mr. Harman, of Throgmorton Street.

To have a creature like this tied to his tail would have made Julius Cæsar ridiculous. One must compassionate Coleridge upon his biographers. They were ridiculous, but not dull. Wordsworth's luck, so humorously described by De Quincey, followed him to the tomb. His biography is un-

readable. Not risible, not absurd, not disappoint-
ing—in the sense of beginning well and then falling
off again—but from first to last, from birth to
death, absolutely impossible. No one has ever
read this Life of Wordsworth. Yet there it is,
decent, clerical, composed, with an admirable portrait. Wordsworth was indeed a lucky fellow.

Gillman's Life of Coleridge, like Hogg's Life of
Shelley, is a fragment. There all resemblance
ceases. It is dull and awkward. The most recent
of Coleridge's biographers, Mr. Ashe, in the new
Aldine Edition of the Poems, has his subject at his
fingers' ends. Mr. Dykes Campbell perhaps might
be able to trip him up over a date, or even to
correct his bibliography, but Mr. Ashe's knowledge
will stand any less severe test. But it has not
engendered reverence. Mr. Ashe raps the author
of " Christabel " pretty sharply over the knuckles
at times. This jars upon me. Petty fault-finding
with the dead is an odious task. Yet what is to be
done ? If there is to be an authoritative and
lengthy Life of Coleridge, what other tone is there
for it to adopt ?

It is impossible, at this distance of time, to be
patronising and admit the public on payment of
thirty-six shillings to two carefully swept volumes

ending with a nicely selected view of the Highgate
Seer as the Christian Philosopher.   The chatter of
half a century, the Cottles and the Allsops, the De
Quinceys and the Carlyles, have put that out of
the question.

How much of Coleridge is still fruitful for man,
and how much has Time put up for ever in his
wallet ?   This is the question the biographer of
Coleridge must ask himself again and again.   It is
a difficult question.   To answer it hastily would be
disrespectful to many distinguished men—mostly
dead men no doubt, but none the less distinguished
on that account.   Many will be found to answer it
by saying the poet, the critic, and the table-talker
live ;   the rest no longer counts.   Some might
insist on adding the leading article writer.

Coleridge's poetry—meaning thereby his best
things—and his criticism, are known to everybody ; but his volume of " Table Talk," though, of
course, well known, is not so widely distributed, so
generally to be found within an arm's length of
everywhere, as it ought to be.   Were we alone on
Salisbury Plain, I would whisper in your ear :
" Coleridge's ' Table-Talk ' is better than Selden's,
more varied than Luther's, almost as readable and
vastly more instructive than Dr. Johnson's."   Mr.

Traill, an excellent judge of a book, pronounces it
" one of the most delightful in the world."

It is (thank Heaven !) entirely free from any
trace of Cottle or of Allsop, and is in no way
reminiscent of Mr. Gillman's back parlour. We
have in it the scholar, the gentleman, the poet, the
politician, the critic, and the theologian, each very
much at his ease. Of course, it is S. T. C. all the
time. " For one mercy I owe thanks beyond all
utterance—that with my gastric and bowel dis-
tempers, my head hath ever been like the head of
a mountain in blue air and sunshine." There is
something piteous in this thankfulness.

> Alas ! the gratitude of men
> Hath oftener left me mourning.

But would my hasty answer be the right one ?
To lop off the philosopher is a bold stroke. Take
down the first volume of Mr. J. S. Mill's " Disserta-
tions and Discussions," and turn to the article
" Coleridge," first published in 1840, six years after
the poet's death. Mill was not a disciple, but with
what solemnity does he write of the master !
" Every Englishman of the present day is by
implication either a Benthamite or a Coleridgian."
" The time is yet far distant when in the estimate
of Coleridge, and of his influence upon the intellect

of our time, anything like unanimity can be looked for." " As a philosopher, the class of thinkers has scarcely yet arisen by whom he is to be judged." These sentences suffice to show that, in Mill's opinion, Coleridge was not merely an influential and suggestive writer, but a great thinker destined to engage the concentrated attention of students for long years to come.

Fifty years have gone since Mill's article, and unless the judgment be that Coleridge was not a philosopher at all, no other has been passed, nor does it look as if one were in course of preparation. Tractarians and nebulous persons have owed Coleridge much, and drunk inspiration at his fountains, but they have passed away to other things than his. The men of philosophy nowadays do not want Coleridge's religion, nor do the men of religion want his philosophy. His " Aids to Reflection " stirred youthful piety, and awoke a new interest in the writings of Archbishop Leighton and other divines of the best period of our Church's history. His views on Bibliolatry made parents uneasy as they heard the " Confessions of an Inquiring Spirit " crudely reproduced at the tea-table by their children. But this is now all ancient history. It would be a task for one wizard to set

another to construct a soul-shelter, warranted to
stand a week's wear and tear, out of the odds and
ends of Coleridgian ways of thought.

If this indeed be so, the Life of Coleridge need
not be a very long one. Perhaps there hardly need
be one at all. Coleridge's best is priceless. This
mortal has put on immortality. Why seek the
living amongst the unbeautiful dead and a sordid
past ? Close your Cottle ; open your " Christabel." Forget De Quincey's spite and Carlyle's
scorn, and read " Kubla Khan," and the next
time you go a railway journey slip the " Table-
Talk " into your pocket.

III.

CARDINAL NEWMAN.

(1890.)

MEN are to be found in these days—bold, bad men, no doubt—ready to declare they have heard enough of the Oxford Movement ; that they resent as affected and overdone the reverential attitude it has become traditional to assume towards it ; that it was (so they may be heard asserting) a short-sighted view of history and tradition ; that it was not even supplied with the tools of research and criticism ; that it never took hold of national thought or feeling, but remained from first to last a magnificent clique ; that it has long since spent itself out, and deserves to be forgotten. It wrote the " Tracts " and edited the " Fathers," but the " Tracts " gather dust upon the shelf, while the " Fathers " have been handed over to the tender mercies of Archdeacon Farrar, in whose hands, naturally enough, they appear more babyish than ever.

This is sheer impatience, even truculent impatience, but it contains a note of warning.

The Oxford Movement has come to as complete an end as anything in this world. Its leader is not only a cardinal of the Roman Church, but the author of a book—" Lectures on Certain Difficulties felt by Anglicans in submitting to the Catholic Church " (1850)—which, in point of style and warm human interest, is worth all the " Tracts " that were ever written, in which he positively pokes fun at the movement, heaps scorn upon the movement, blows the movement from the mouth of an oratorical cannon, loaded, as only he knows how to load such a cannon, up to the very nose with arguments so varied, illustrations so enlightening, pleading so tender, sarcasm so biting, that, when the book is closed, the reader does not so much as cast a glance round for fragments of the movement ; he knows the movement has for ever disappeared. So far as I am aware, no reply was attempted to this onslaught. Newman was allowed to slay his own child in silence. It is seldom such a spectacle is witnessed as a man turning in intellectual scorn upon his former self, and raking out the holes in which he once found shelter. Newman did it mercilessly, and therefore effectually. He cut down the trees and the rooks returned no more.

In considering the Cardinal's hold upon English literature, we must be as remorseless as he was himself, and cut ourselves adrift from the Oxford Movement, and even—to some extent, at least—from the pulpit of St. Mary's. We must forget the retreat at Littlemore. It may seem ungracious to do this, and, in our milder moods, it is certainly hard. The memories of those days are most musical, most melancholy, to all who possess them ; whilst those who possess no memories find an aroma clinging to the bare records of a time when taste, temper, and poetry presided over the cauldron of religious controversy. The history of religious thought and emotion in this country is usually so harsh and crude that, when it is the contrary of all this, we prize its memory.

But as time goes on it will become more and more difficult and at last impossible to recall the past, and to reproduce artificially the very peculiar and non-natural atmosphere that surrounded the Oxford Movement. It will become stranger and stranger, the beauties will seem less beautiful, and the oddities still odder. Even the " Apologia " itself will puzzle more than please.

Newman's great literary characteristics, that placed him in the very forefront of English authors, his force, his fancy, his oratorical rush upon his opponent, are not to be looked for in the " Apologia " (1864), or in the " Essay of Development " (1845), or in the " History of the Arians " (1833), or even in the " Parochial Sermons " (1837–1842), things of beauty—cold beauty—as those are, but in the books he has written since his mind has swung at ease in the anchorage of Rome, since he cast off the restraints of an awkward attitude ; in his " Lectures on the Present Position of Catholics in England " (1851), in his " Lectures on Anglican Difficulties " (1850), in his three books on " University Teaching " (1852–1856–1859), in his " Sermons to Mixed Congregations " (1850), in his " Discussions and Arguments " (1872).

The contrast between the Anglican and the Catholic writer is enormous. It is like the meeting of great waters. The one restrained, at times uneasy, eminently unpopular, remote from the trodden paths of feeling ; the other exuberant, though never redundant, triumphant, sometimes to the pitch of boisterousness, sweeps along, marshalling forces, polishing epigrams, and making appeals, no longer to the scholar and theologian and prim church-goer, but to the man in the street—the rank and file of humanity.

In reading these writings of Cardinal Newman's, the great quality which first manifests itself is his splendid fancy. In the actual, positive restraint which he places upon the exuberant energy of this gift or faculty he shows himself the artist. Sometimes it runs away with him; usually it is his servant, not his master. But his readers are not conscious of the curb—they believe themselves to be revelling and rioting, whilst in reality they are being driven steadily along.

The subjects which delight Dr. Newman are not theological or purely philosophical subjects, but those mixed questions of history and morals and probabilities which really enter into men's minds and form the staple of their beliefs, prejudices, and prepossessions.

In dealing with subjects of this kind, this scholar and celibate, this " pilgrim pale with Paul's sad girdle bound," glows with all the enthusiasm and employs all the devices of the greatest of advocates, displays the knowledge and appositeness of the most accomplished man of the world, and winds himself in and out of his subject with the finished ease of a great leader of parliamentary debate. To prove these words, if proof be needed, would be easy enough were space for half a dozen quotations at our disposal. It is not, but I will press upon any reader as yet in ignorance (which is an unblessed state) of the general run of the Cardinal's writings since he cast off his Anglicanism to read the " Lectures on the Present Position of Catholics in England." The feeling excited by their perusal will be one of mingled amazement and delight—amazement at their enormous force, and delight in their consummate literary skill and artifice.

These lectures are an admirable example of Dr. Newman's favourite method. They are not concerned with the truth of Catholicism, they do not even deny in terms the truth of Protestantism. Logically, their effect would remain the same had they been written by, let us say, Dr. Maitland or Mr. Rose.* It is apparently a light-hearted book, written in tremendous spirits, bubbling over with fun, decorated with countless fancies—yet what was the task it set itself to perform ? Nothing less than this, to roll back the great Protestant

* Mr. Rose was the " original begetter " of the " Oxford Movement." Mr. Rose was a Cambridge man.

tradition, of the court, the law, of society, and literature ; to remove whole mountains of prejudice ; to cleanse the Protestant mind of all the slimy traces of slander ; to shiver in pieces the prejudices of centuries ; and to let the old faith of Englishmen stand forth as a body of doctrine and rule of life. What a task ! Protestants though we are, we can scarce forbear to cheer. The mastery displayed by Dr. Newman in grappling with it is beyond praise, and without precedent. He is all that Burke is, and genuinely playful besides. He successfully conceals the prodigious effort he is making and the enormous importance of the verdict for which he is striving. An abler book it would be impossible to name.

Another quality of these writings is their warm colouring and glow. They are full of life and movement. As we read we hear the

> Murmur of Living
> Stir of Existence,
> Soul of the World.

Take down from the shelf the " Discourses to Mixed Congregations," and read the sixth, entitled " God's Will the End of Life," with its picture of " this vain, unprofitable, yet overbearing world," of its shops and newspapers, " discoveries in art and science, discoveries (so-called) in religion, the court, royalty, the entertainments of the great places of amusement, strange trials, offences, accidents, escapes, exploits, experiments, contests, ventures. Oh, this curious, restless, clamorous, panting being which we call life!" Turn back a few pages, and you may find yourself reading :

> Alas! poor soul, and whilst it thus fights (after death) with that destiny which it has brought upon itself, and those companions whom it has chosen, the man's name perhaps is solemnly chanted forth, and his memory decently cherished among his friends on earth. His readiness in speech, his fertility in thought, his sagacity, or his wisdom are not forgotten. Men talk of him from time to time : they appeal to his authority ; they quote his words ; perhaps they even raise a monument to his name or write his history. "So comprehensive a mind! Such a power of throwing light on a perplexed subject and bringing conflicting ideas or facts into harmony." "Such a speech it was that he made on such and such an occasion ; I happened to be present, and never shall forget it " ; or "It was the saying of a very sensible man " ; or "A great personage, whom some of us knew " ; or "Never was his equal in society, so just in his remarks, so lively, so versatile, so unobtrusive " ; or "I was fortunate to see him once when I was a boy." "His discoveries so great " ; or "His philosophy so profound." O vanity, vanity of vanities! All is vanity.

And then he concludes with five words I cannot bring myself to transcribe.

Throughout the length and breadth of Dr. Newman's Catholic writings is to be noticed this alertness for humanity, this quickness of eye and ear. He cares little for the abstract, for theory, for treatises and disquisitions, even for theology. His great dread is Atheism, a foe of whom he never speaks save with bated breath. How may mankind best be saved from Atheism ? This question is for ever sounding in his ears. This eminently practical way of looking at things gives a unity to his numerous writings. You soon learn what he will be at, and how questions will strike him. This is to know an author when you know beforehand not what he will say, but how he will set about saying it.

It must not be inferred from anything that has been said that Cardinal Newman's interest in humanity has made him a democrat. There is certainly nothing in his writings to show any admiration for the common people. Hartley Coleridge once wrote an essay to prove Shakespeare a Tory—there is material for an essay to prove Newman one.

Amongst the most magnificent of Dr. Newman's writings must be included his " Lectures on the Scope and Extension of University Education." They are not in accord with dominant notions, but if the opinions there expounded, enforced, and illustrated are indeed dead, never did dead opinions lie more richly enshrined.

I am not here concerned with the truth or false-hood of Dr. Newman's position. We are consider-ing him as a great author, as a master of " the thought and the word, distinct but inseparable from each other." He himself has said :

And since the thoughts and reasoning of an author have a personal character, no wonder that his style is not only the image of his subject, but of his mind. That pomp of language, that full and tuneful diction, that felicitousness in the choice and exquisiteness in the collocation of words which to prosaic writers seem artificial, is nothing else but the mere habit and way of a lofty intellect.

What Dr. Newman wrote of others may be said of him. That style of his, what is it but the mere habit and way of a lofty intelligence ? It is this and more ; it is also the reflex of a spirit which, though at times, when carried away by his rhetoric, fierce and unforgiving, is yet a benignant spirit.

But though not concerned with truth, I am sorely reluctant to leave Dr. Newman with nothing better on my lips or more enduring on my mind than praises of his style. This perpetual twaddle about style is becoming just a little sickening. After all, the thought is the thing. When a great writer has a great style, we may—and in the case of Dr. Newman we do—thank God for the union ; when, as in the case of Bishop Butler, the style is lacking, we need only say it is a pity ; but when some starveling intellect prates about his cadences one longs for cudgels.

I therefore bring these few remarks to a close by quoting a famous passage from the Cardinal's letter to the Duke of Norfolk (1875) :

"This, at least, is how I read the doctrine of Protestants as well as of Catholics. The rule and measure of duty is not utility, nor expedience, nor the happiness of the greatest number, nor State convenience, nor fitness, order, and the *pulchrum*. Conscience is not a longsighted selfishness, nor a desire to be consistent with oneself, but it is a messenger from Him who, both in nature and in grace, speaks to us behind a veil, and teaches and rules us by His representatives. Conscience is the aboriginal vicar of Christ, a prophet in its informations, a monarch in its peremptoriness, a priest in its blessings and anathemas, and, even though the eternal priesthood throughout the Church could cease to be, in it the sacerdotal principle would remain and would have a sway."

This is noble English, sound morality, and (I hope) good Roman doctrine.

IV.

MISS FERRIER.*

(1898.)

THIS is a dour book, not a little reminiscent of the wind-swept streets, stony, brass-plated houses of the "gray metropolis of the North," where, though be it remembered in the "old town," Miss Ferrier was born in 1782. Her father was Sir Walter Scott's colleague in the clerkship of the Session House, and when he died, in his eighty-sixth year, Scott wrote :

Honest old Mr. Ferrier is dead at extreme old age. I confess I should not wish to live so long. He was a man of strong passions and strong prejudices, but with generous and manly sentiments at the same time.

Old Mr. Ferrier seems a familiar type of Scot. As life advanced he became deeply religious, and devoted much time to the reading of the Bible in the Authorised Version. By the death of her brother and the marriages of her sisters, Susan

* "Memoirs and Correspondence of Susan Ferrier." (London : John Murray.)

Ferrier early became the mistress of her father's
house. She was dark and tall, though not handsome, a good talker, and the centre, so we are told,
of a brilliant coterie in Edinburgh. Supper was
the prevailing meal, and it certainly has a pleasant
sound about it. We are almost prepared to believe
in the brilliance of a coterie that included a
number of women who talked unconventionally
and who supped freely. Otherwise we are apt to
be sceptical about the " brilliance " of bygone
parties, whether in Paris, London, Boston, or
Edinburgh. One bore will ruin any party, and at
most parties there is apt to be at least one bore.
Strong-minded old ladies, who called a spade a
spade and wondered what ailed Joseph at Poti-
phar's wife, flourished in the old town of Edinburgh *circa* 1800. These ladies dressed and spoke
and did exactly as they chose ; they were witty,
outspoken, and eccentric, and most excellent company. They have lingered with us during this
century, but the next will know them no more.
They were pious, though often profane ; pure-
minded, though not infrequently coarse ; splendid
story-tellers, kind of heart, though sharp of
tongue, and they feared the face of no son of
Adam, and never set their caps at any man. As

companions they were excellent, and as maiden
aunts adorable. Peace to their ashes! Miss
Susan Ferrier knew many such dames, and, to
some extent at all events, they live and move in
the pages of her three novels.

As for these three novels, it is perhaps enough
to say that they delighted some of the best judges
of Scotch tales that ever lived. Many clever
women, who knew Scotland and Scottish character and Scottish habits outside and in, numbered
" Marriage," " The Inheritance," and " Destiny "
as among the best of their kind. I was brought up
to regard them with favour, and some of the
strongest motives that prompt mankind still urge
me to extol them as of the first order. Devoutly
as I hope that they are indeed classics, I cannot
conceal from myself that I notice stealing over
them what looks suspiciously like the hues of old
age, decay, and death. A great deal of them is
written in a style which does not obviously defy
time—there are long, dreary bits in all three
novels, and altogether I tremble. Miss Ferrier
must be compared with Miss Burney and Miss
Edgeworth—to pit her against Miss Austen
is as absurd as to couple anybody with
Shakespeare. Miss Ferrier is quite as good as Miss

Burney, and has some advantages over Miss Edgeworth. But books do not live by comparisons, but
by their pleasure-giving qualities.

Miss Ferrier was no mean letter-writer :

And to set you an example, I am going to tell you that I am
deeply and desperately in love. And what makes my case
particularly deplorable is that there is not the least prospect
of the dear man lending so much as a little finger to pull me
out of the mire into which he has plunged me. Were I possessed
of the same mean spirit of bartering as you, I'd have you guess
his degree, but you'd as soon bethink you of the great Cham of
Tartary as the Right Honourable John Philpot Curran, Master
of the Rolls, Ireland ! ! ! I wish I could give you any idea of
his charms, but alas ! my pen does not, like Rousseau's, *brûle
sur le papier,* and none but a pen of fire could trace his character
or record the charms of his conversation. He had the cruelty
to tell me he liked me, and then he left me. Had my eyes been
worth a button, they'd soon have settled the matter, but
there's the misery of being sent into the world with such mussel
shells ! ! I (a modest maiden) said nothing, and it seems they
were silent, and so we parted, never to meet again ! ! !

But though a lively writer of the old Scottish,
who does not shrink from a good story because the
word " bastard " crops up in it, and who can speak
of Eve sporting her green Dickie, Miss Ferrier
sticks to it that a *good moral* cannot be dispensed
with in a work of fiction :

But as the only good purpose of a book is to inculcate
morality, and convey some lesson of instruction as well as
delight, I do not see that what is called a *good moral* can be
dispensed with in a work of fiction.

This being so, it is not so surprising as it otherwise would be to find that Miss Ferrier actually

enjoyed " Cœlebs in Search of a Wife." She hated
Cœlebs, it is true. So far, good ; but she adds,
" The Stanley family are delightful upon paper."
Delightful ! What a word to apply to such woeful
matter. How hard it is to be a critic !

Miss Ferrier, though shy of publicity, had a
great mind to be an author. She sends her charming friend, Miss Clavering, a rough sketch of
" Marriage " in these words :

Now, as to my own deeds, I shall make no apologies for
sending you a hasty and imperfect sketch of what I think
might be wrought up to a tolerable form. I do not recollect
ever to have seen the sudden transition of a high-bred English
beauty who thinks she can sacrifice all for love to an uncomfortable Highland dwelling among tall, red-haired sisters and
grim aunts. Don't you think this would make a good opening
of the piece ? Suppose each of us to try our hands upon it !
The moral to be deduced is to warn all young ladies against
runaway matches, and the characters and fates of the two
sisters would be *unexceptionable.* I expect it will be the first
book every wise matron will put into the hand of her daughter,
and even the reviewers will relax of their severity in favour of
the morality of this little work. Enchanting sight ! Already
do I behold myself arrayed in an old mouldy covering, thumbed
and creased and filled with dog's-ears. I hear the enchanting
sound of some sentimental miss, the shrill pipe of some
antiquated spinster, or the hoarse grumbling of some married
dowager as they severally inquire for me at the circulating
library. Child, child, you had need be sensible of the value
of my correspondence !

After this pleasant, easy-going fashion did the
novelists of the last century produce their wares.

They wished to amuse and do a little good ; and, if possible, make a little money.

Miss Ferrier took naturally to writing :

For know that I am descended from a race of scribes. I was born amidst briefs and deeds. I was nurtured upon ink—my pap-spoon was the stump of an old pen, my christening robe was a reclaiming petition, and my cradle a paper-poke !

This early familiarity gave her writing from the first an assurance and grasp which, had her literary traditions only been a little sounder, might have secured her a longevity hardly likely to be hers. Still, however that may be, and it is perhaps idle to predict, Miss Ferrier was and must ever remain a considerable writer.

I cannot say that this record of her life, apart from many lively letters of Miss Ferrier's own, is very interesting. In fact, I have found it a little depressing. None the less, it is a true book.

" Marriage " appeared in 1818, " The Inheritance " in 1824, " Destiny " in 1830. In 1841 they all appeared in Bentley's Standard Edition of Novels, a blessed series, containing the books not only of Miss Ferrier and Miss Austen, but of Peacock ! In 1852, Bentley republished Miss Ferrier's novels, and for the first time her name appeared on their title pages. She died in 1854, and lies buried in St. Cuthbert's Church, Edinburgh.

V.

" ELEMENTARY JANE."

(*The Times*, June, 1922.) *

It is always with a shiver of apprehension that the true lover of a celebrated author learns that there is impending the publication of some hitherto unknown works, whether of youth or age, of the author in question. What will they be like, and how will they fit in with those already known by heart ? are questions hardly to be asked without some measure of trepidation.

Especially is this the case when the prevailing note of the author's already published work is perfection. There are writers, and distinguished ones, to whom this shrinking dread does not apply. De Quincey, for example; did we hear that a whole parcel of his manuscript had been found in a cupboard in Edinburgh, we should feel no

* " Love and Freindship : and other Early Works now First Printed." By Jane Austen. With a Preface by G. K. Chesterton. (Chatto & Windus, 1922.)

qualms, for he is already so " multifarious " and
unequal an author that a dozen or so more of his
writings could make no difference ; and it may be
so with Hazlitt, or even, perhaps, with Shakespeare. But Miss Austen is another matter. We
have already had some dubious experiences, and
though " Lady Susan " and the " Watsons " are
things we can put up with, we could have been
quite content to have been left alone with
" Emma " and the other five.

It was therefore with fear and trembling that
I found myself handling for the first time this
dainty volume, and learnt from the short preface
contributed by Mr. Chesterton that its contents
are believed to have been written by Jane Austen
in her seventeenth year. As a general rule, we can
do without the pen-productions of " sweet seventeen," but the first four pages of " Love and
Freindship " dissipated all our fears, and we found
ourselves simply revelling in the revelation there
made to us of the " Elementary Jane," and
entirely in agreement with Mr. Chesterton, who
remarks in his preface that these fragments " are
something more than the discovery of a document ; it is the discovery of an inspiration. And
that inspiration was the inspiration of Gargantua

and Pickwick, it was the gigantic inspiration of laughter."

Mr. Chesterton has his own heightened fashion of saying things, and he hardly carries me with him when he goes on to say that Jane Austen could have been a buffoon like the Wife of Bath if she chose, but about the revelation and the elementary " inspiration " he seems to me to have hit the nail on the head.

The first story, " Love and Freindship," is told in fifteen letters which introduce us, in an exceeding short space, to quite a crowd of characters. The letters are written by Laura to Marianne, the youthful daughter of an old friend, in order that their recipient may marvel at the afflictions and admire the fortitude of the writer. The third letter begins thus :

My father was a native of Ireland and an inhabitant of Wales. My mother was the natural daughter of a Scotch peer by an Italian opera girl. I was born in Spain, and received my education at a convent in France.

Very unlike the staid Emma and her father. Then we have Laura's father and mother depicted in a few inimitable touches, and the " Noble Youth," Edward, with whom Laura incontinently fell in love at first sight, and to whom she was " immediately united by her father, who, tho' he had never taken Orders, had been bred to the Church." Strange writing this for a parson's daughter of seventeen, and but for a reasonable doubt whether a copy of " John Buncle " could ever have found its way into the country rectory of the Rev. George Austen, I could have sworn that the " Elementary Jane," ere she penned the words last quoted, had surreptitiously become acquainted with the " English Rabelais," for by this time the reader of this notice will have perceived that " Love and Freindship " is, in Mr. Chesterton's words, " a rattling burlesque."

After Laura's uncanonical marriage with Edward, the penniless pair departed to the house of Edward's sister Augusta, who received them coldly.

A short conversation between Augusta and her brother which I accidentally overheard increased my dislike to her, and convinced me that her heart was no more formed for the soft ties of Love than for endearing intercourse of Friendship.

" But do you think that my father will ever be reconciled to this imprudent connection ? " said Augusta.

" Augusta," replied the noble youth, " I thought you had a better opinion of me than to imagine I would so abjectly degrade myself as to consider my father's concurrence in any of my affairs, either of consequence or concern to me. Tell me, Augusta, tell me with sincerity, did you ever know me consult his inclination or follow his advice in the least trifling particular since the age of fifteen ? "

" Edward," replied she, " you are surely too diffident in

your own praise. Since you were fifteen only ! My dear brother, since you were five years old I entirely acquit you of ever having willingly contributed to the satisfaction of your father. But I am still not without apprehension of your being shortly obliged to degrade yourself in your own eyes by seeking a support for your wife in the generosity of Sir Edward."

"Never, never, Augusta, will I so demean myself," said Edward. "Support! What support will Laura want which she can receive from him ? "

" Only these very insignificant ones, of victuals and drink," answered she.

" Victuals and Drink ! " replied my husband in a most nobly contemptuous manner ; " and dost thou, then, imagine that there is no other support for an exalted mind (such as is my Laura's) than the mean and indelicate employment of eating and drinking ? "

" None that I know of so efficacious," returned Augusta.

Where on earth did this child of seventeen pick up this finished style in a very difficult *genre ?*   It is almost a portent.

I had intended, in order to give myself the pleasure of introducing the other characters of this amazing tale, to pursue it to its close, but on reflection I perceived that to do so would be an act of cruelty to the reader by robbing him of his just dues.

At times the tone of the tale is undeniably harsh, and it may be crude, and the sarcasm almost too cutting. More than once, whilst reading " Love and Freindship," the exclamation rose to my lips :

So young, and so untender.

But it was a foolish exclamation to make, for the whole thing is conceived, brought forth, and completed by the author in a spirit of sheer delight in finding herself (whilst holding her pen) in full possession and control of high spirits, an exuberant fancy and the glorious sense of fun. To think of " Love and Freindship " otherwise is to think of it wrongly.

The other story, " Lesley Castle," also told in letters, remains unfinished, and is in the same burlesque vein throughout.

" The History of England from the reign of Henry the 4th to the death of Charles the 1st. By a partial, prejudiced and ignorant historian," is a little harder to explain. It is not a burlesque, though comically composed, and the young historian certainly deserves all the epithets she so freely bestows upon herself, for she is partial, prejudiced and ignorant with a vengeance, but to what extent she is representing her own opinions you cannot say. She proclaims herself a furious Yorkist and a sworn adherent of the House of Stuart. Mary Queen of Scots is pronounced a blameless heroine, whilst Queen Elizabeth is damned as furiously as she ever was by another damsel of genius, who, however, never lived

to come to maturity, Marjorie Fleming. She
makes one thing very plain, however—her early
and enduring passion for the profession of a
sailor.

On the whole one cannot express one's feelings
for this very remarkable little book better than by
adopting Mr. Chesterton's words :

" There is a larger critical reason for taking
pleasure in the gaiety of these various travesties
and trifles. Mr. Austen-Leigh seems to have
thought them not sufficiently serious for the
reputation of his great relative; but greatness is
not made up of serious things in the sense of
solemn things. The reason here, however, is as
serious as even he or any one else could desire,
for it concerns the fundamental quality of one of
the finest talents in letters."

VI.

THE WISDOM OF OUR ANCESTORS AND THE DRINK TRAFFIC.

(1893.)

BUNG, or Boniface—call him which you will—and his many friends are not, whatever may be their other merits, reading men, and it is therefore by no means surprising that they should, in this hour of their distress, jump to the conclusion that abhorrence of them and of the traffic in strong drink is a new thing born into the world with Sir Wilfrid Lawson, Canon Wilberforce, Lady Henry Somerset, and the United Kingdom'Alliance. Publican, brewer, and distiller, whether peers of Parliament, like Bass and Allsopp and Guinness, or their miserable mortgagors, bound hand and foot by enslaving covenants, and trading with their mortgagee's money, would wish us to understand that in the good old days the drink traffic was encouraged and petted, and that it is only a modern teetotal craze which would expose it to

pains and penalties. A very slight acquaintance
with the history of our licensing laws is sufficient
to knock this delusion on the head. Our sturdy
ancestors, as the phrase runs, knew perfectly well
that where there is strong drink there is danger,
and even in those comparatively sober days, when
the only intoxicating drinks consumed in "Merry
England" were ale, beer, mum, perry, and cider,
and when brandy, gin, rum, and whiskey were as
unknown as in Paradise, even then, all inns,
hostelries, and places of public entertainment had
to be licensed by justices of the peace, and could
only be carried on by men of sobriety, substance,
and repute. A Liverpool gin-shop of to-day, as
carried on by a distiller's mortgagor, where no
food is sold or stabling provided for a traveller's
beast, but which exists only for the sale of fire-
water to an impoverished neighbourhood, would
fare badly if the renewal of its annual poison
licence depended upon the votes of a bench of
fourteenth-century magistrates.

The introduction of spirits into this country is
not a thing of antiquity. Until the reign of George
II. as few people had tasted distilled waters, as
they were called, as had tasted tea, but early in
the eighteenth century the accursed thing became

known and largely indulged in. Spirits were hawked about the streets, and sold on ships up the river, in sheds and stalls. Horrible scenes ensued, and our ancestors at once proceeded to do their best to put them down with the strong arm of the law. The first statute was passed in the year 1729, and forbade the sale of " compound waters or spirits " except by licensed retailers, who were to pay £20 a year for their licences, which required annual renewal. This statute proved difficult to enforce. Informers were handled roughly by the mob, who were free traders in drink, and in 1733 it was repealed, but the sale of spirits was forbidden except in dwelling-houses. Under this law great excesses were perpetrated, and a strong feeling arose in the country, far stronger even than exists at the present day, that the whole traffic was hellish and detrimental to the best interests of the nation, and that it ought to be suppressed once for all. This opinion was entertained not merely by the pious, but by statesmen in both Houses, by lawyers and by authors.* Unfortunately, at the same time thirst

---

* " There should be total suppression of ale-houses, except where it is necessary for the accommodation of travellers." Lord Shelburne, 1785. See Lord Edmund Fitzmaurice's Life, Vol. III., p. 436.

arose in the breasts of our governors, a thirst
which has never yet been quenched, and is as far
from being quenched as ever, the desire for
revenue. Here was a thing—namely, strong drink
—admittedly accursed. In 1730 we had not grown
accustomed to spirits. They still shocked us, but
what was to be done ? Suppress them or tax
them ? It was the parting of the ways. Our
ancestors decided to denounce the traffic, to heap
indignities upon it, but to keep it alive for the
purposes of revenue. And what a revenue has
been extracted from it ! How often have we
not drunk ourselves out of our difficulties !

The celebrated Act of 1736 has the following
preamble :

> Whereas the drinking of spirituous liquors and strong waters
> is become very common, especially among the people of lower
> and inferior rank, the constant and excessive use whereof tends
> greatly to the destruction of their health, renders them unfit
> for useful labour and business, debasing their morals and
> making them to perpetrate all manner of vice ; and the ill
> consequences of the excessive use of such liquors are not con-
> fined to the present generation, but extend to future ages, and
> tend to the devastation and ruin of this kingdom.

Here is a preamble indeed—a sermon some
might call it. This Act, which enumerates
amongst strong drinks brandy, rum, arrack,
usquebaugh, Geneva, and *aqua-vitæ*, forbade their

sale in less quantities than two gallons, except by annually licensed retailers, who were also required to be the proprietors of inns or ale-houses. This annual licence cost £50, a very considerable sum in those days. In 1742 the subject again revived. There can be no doubt the law of 1736 was systematically disregarded—at all events, in London, where spirits were sold by unlicensed retailers, who, so we are assured, were impudent enough to set up painted boards inviting people to be drunk at the small expense of a penny, and at the same time assuring them they might be dead drunk for twopence, and have straw for nothing. The desire for revenue in the year of Dettingen was also strong, and accordingly an Act was passed imposing a new duty per gallon at the still-head, reducing the annual licence from £50 to £1. On the credit of this Act the Ministry immediately borrowed a large sum of money at £3 per cent.

The policy of this measure was furiously debated in that now peaceful Tory club, the House of Lords, where it was clearly perceived that the question was one between public morality and public revenue. We have a report of these debates which we now know to be the work of Samuel

Johnson, who did not hear a word of them, but invented all the speeches on both sides in a garret in Exeter Street, Strand. Lord Chesterfield took part in the debate on the temperance side, and we may read in his collected works the speeches he is supposed to have delivered on those occasions, but though no doubt he did make excellent speeches, he is not responsible for a line of either of those so attributed to him, which are throughout unadulterated Samuel. But for our purposes Johnson is as good as any possible peer of the realm, and our teetotal friends would be greatly solaced if, between the dates of the publication of the *Alliance News*, they turned to this report, which they will find in any edition of Johnson's works which contains the two volumes of Parliamentary Debates.

Lord Hervey is made to say :

The Bill now before you, my Lords, is fundamentally wrong, as it is formed upon a hateful project of increasing the consumption of strong drink, and consequently of promoting drunkenness among a people already reproached for it throughout the whole world. . . . I am, for my part, convinced that drunkards as well as thieves are made by opportunity.

In Lord Chesterfield's mouth the following words are put :

To pretend, my Lords, that the design of this Bill is to prevent or diminish the use of spirits is to trample upon common sense, for when did any man hear that a commodity was prohibited by licensing its sale, or that to offer and refuse is the same action. They are resolved, my Lords, that the nation, which nothing can make wise, shall, while they are at its head, at least be merry.

Lord Lonsdale is credited with the following :

Such, my Lords, is at present the state of the nation ; twelve millions of gallons of these poisonous liquors are every year swallowed by the inhabitants of this kingdom, and this quantity, enormous as it is, will probably every year increase.

Johnson makes most of his temperance orators denounce in glowing passages, too long for quotation, the folly of raising money for the maintenance of a war out of the demoralisation of the people, and on the whole it must, we think, be admitted that he takes care throughout his report that the drunken dogs should get the worst of the argument. The Act passed, though ten prelates—to their honour be it said—voted against it.

I cannot now pursue the subject any further. Act has always followed Act in an unbroken succession, and at the present moment, though scores have been repealed, there are still thirty-eight statutes in force in England alone relating to this trade, which Mr. Joseph Chamberlain has pronounced the chief industry of the country. From first to last it has been a suspected trade, which has only been tolerated for purposes of taxation.

VII.

THE HISTORICAL SENSE.

(*The Times*, 1922.)

I HAVE often thought what a good thing it would be if the curricula of our theological colleges, to whatever profession of faith they are attached, could be so framed as to render it necessary for their students to read the favourite history books of their opponents ; not, of course, in substitution for their own pet authorities, but in addition to and by way of comment thereupon.

What better training could there be for a future Anglican rector, vicar, or curate in charge of a country parish than to have become acquainted in his early days of study with such records of piety and devotion (however tinged with error) as are to be found in books such as Calamy's historical account of his own life (1671–1731), or the same author's " Nonconformists' Memorial "—" being an account of the lives, sufferings, and printed works of the two thousand ministers ejected from the Church of England by the Act of Uniformity, 1662," or even such a work as Walter Wilson's " History and Antiquities of Dissenting Churches and Meeting Houses in London, Westminster, and Southwark, including the Lives of their Ministers " ?

From the pages of these books the future Anglican divine would learn that Nonconformity has its religious history no less than the Anglican Church, can venerate the memory of its own martyrs and confessors, and appeal to a noble tradition deeply ingrained and channelled into the religious life of England.

On the other hand, what could be better for the inmates of a dissenting college than early to become aware of the existence of that once-famous folio with a title too long to be here inserted, which the second-hand booksellers of to-day curtly paraphrase as " Walker's Sufferings of the Clergy in the Times of the Great Rebellion," and sometimes even more curtly as " Walker's Sufferings " ?

It is a pity to see priests, parsons, and ministers go through life with an historical sense either mutilated or perhaps even never aroused. The historical sense is based on an intelligent curiosity to find out what really happened long ago, and how

it came about that men and women, fashioned like
ourselves, treated one another in the way they did.
This can only be found out by reading all round a
subject, and is perhaps more likely to be discovered in biography than in what is called history.

Some sixty years ago I used occasionally to meet
at my father's table some excellent Liverpool men
who were wont at times, after supper, to expand
with pride as they recalled the fact that they could
claim descent from divines recorded in Calamy's
" Nonconformist Memorial " as having been
ejected from their Church of England livings in
August, 1662. But with the statement of this
regrettable occurrence their interest in the matter
seemed altogether to cease, for they could never
tell me how it was that their godly ancestors
were in possession of those livings in August,
1662. Who were their immediate predecessors ?
Walker's " Sufferings " was not in my father's
library—where Calamy reigned supreme—but as
I had access (*laus deo*) to the fine lending library
attached to the Liverpool " Lyceum," I had no
difficulty in discovering " Walker," and then,
aided by the excellent index of names to be found
at the end of that fascinating volume, to make out
for myself how, in some instances at all events,

these ancestors of my father's friends came to be
in possession of the livings from which they were
cruelly ejected. It was by the simple process of
turning out their predecessors. A Puritan curate
took the place (sometimes rather shabbily) of what
we should now call a High Church vicar. When I
carried this information to my father's friends and
offered to make extracts from " Walker " about
their ancestors, I was not well received, and was
once bidden " to beware of the knowledge that
puffeth up."

In suggesting this course of reading to all sides
alike—Catholic, Anglican, Nonconformist—it is
not within the compass of my imagination that,
e.g., a good Catholic, with a real hold upon his
faith, would ever come to be disturbed in it by
reading Hallam, Macaulay, or even Foxe's " Book
of Martyrs," any more than a sound Protestant
would be likely to be upset in his settled conviction
as to the right of private judgment by reading
Lingard's " History of England." Nothing of the
kind would happen, but of this one may well be
certain, that a vast amount of historical prejudice
would be dissipated in the process, and who would
not wish to get quit once for all of historical
prejudice ?

Quite apart from the educational advantage in the training of the clergy and ministers of all denominations, the mere reader of English history can never hope to reap the full fruits of that delightful pursuit unless he puts up his game in all the coverts, and studies both sides of the great controversies—King or Commonwealth, Pope or Queen.

There was a time, not so very long ago, when the ordinary boy or girl brought up in a Protestant household (who need wish to be brought up anywhere else ?) had but little chance of doing justice to the Catholic side of the terrible quarrel of the sixteenth century.

How few of us sixty years ago had even so much as heard of Father Campion, whose biography by Richard Simpson is now one of the most exciting as well as soul-stirring of English biographies. We knew a good deal about Archbishop Cranmer, but next to nothing of his successor, Reginald Pole, who was consecrated at Greenwich a day after Cranmer had been burnt in Oxford. Now it will be generally admitted that, as men to read about, Pole is at least as interesting and a great deal more cosmopolitan than Cranmer.

The collections of Father Morris, S.J., published

in three volumes under the title of " The Troubles of our Catholic Forefathers," Father Foley's long series, called " Records of the English Province of the Society of Jesus," and the writings of those two learned priests, Fathers Bridgett and Knox, have opened up to the curious reader, who really wants to know how things happened as they did, wide fields hitherto unexplored save by the most learned of historical students.

Dom Bede Camm's book is a very pleasing example of the kind of history I am constrained to recommend to the Protestant reader.

" Forgotten Shrines " * is a happy mixture of a guide book for pedestrians and motorists when in search of the picturesque and of an historical story-book for those who love to recall the past.

" Forgotten Shrines " is, of course, a Roman Catholic book, and is composed in a spirit of devotion and affectionate regard for those brave men and women, the adherents in terrible times of the old religion ; but it does not deal with points of doctrine, and contains nothing likely to ruffle any one's theological feathers.

It begins by taking us to Norbury Hall, on the

---

* " Forgotten Shrines." By Dom Bede Camm. (The *Tablet* Office, Henrietta Street, Covent Garden.)

Dove, in Derbyshire, built by Sir Henry Fitzherbert at the beginning of the fourteenth century,
and in later days inhabited by that famous judge,
Sir Anthony Fitzherbert, the author of one of the
rarest of English law books (1516), " La Graunde
Abridgement." Sir Anthony was a devout
Catholic and a truly pious man, but he lived in
times when it was hard for a Catholic judge to
steer clear of heresy, and he was compelled to be
a member of the tribunal that tried Fisher and
More—a terrible blot on any escutcheon, Catholic
or Protestant. Under the picturesque title " A
Ruined Castle by the Sea," our author takes us on
a pilgrimage to Warblington Castle, and here we
are told the tale of Margaret Countess of Salisbury,
the mother of Reginald Pole, the friend and
governess of Mary Tudor, and at last, when nearly
seventy, the murdered victim of Henry VIII.,
aided and abetted by both Houses of Parliament.
A visit to Markenfield Hall, near Ripon, enables
the writer *renovare dolorem* of the second pilgrimage of grace—and so on, down a long list of castles,
parks, and halls. The very numerous illustrations, taken chiefly from photographs made on
the spot by the pilgrim himself, all add to the
romance.

Turning over the pages of this beautiful book, it was borne in upon me that the balance, once so heavily weighted against the Catholic side in our history, has now begun to kick the beam the other way. It is time that some equally picturesque pen should tell us " sad stories " of the martyrs and confessors whose names are enshrined in the " Nonconformists' Memorial " and elsewhere. I am afraid the camera would not be of so much assistance to the compiler of those tales as it has been to Dom Bede Camm. " The Troubles of our Puritan Forefathers " were mostly endured in towns ; but a picturesque pen ought to be able to make a back-parlour in Aldermanbury or Norwich as moving a scene for great actions of courage and devotion as an old hall or even a moated grange. But when I ask myself, what would " Forgotten Shrines " be without its illustrations ? I feel a little doubtful about this, but the experiment should certainly be made, by somebody else.

Stripped of all its horrible accessories, the stake for the Protestant, the axe for the Catholic, cruel imprisonments and torture for both, the issue presented to our forefathers in the time of Queen Elizabeth was the simple one—was England to be a Protestant or a Roman Catholic country ; and hid within the kernel of this issue was another one, wholly unrecognised at the time—namely, the issue between authority in the matter of religion and complete freedom of opinion.

As to the determination of this momentous issue, it may perhaps be questioned whether a close historical study of records and biography will aid us very much in making up our own minds one way or the other, but from the humanitarian point of view, and for getting rid of vulgar prejudice, the more we read the more tolerant we must become.

VIII.

BYRON'S LETTERS.

(*The Times*, February, 1922.)

Two more volumes of Byron's correspondence have been added to the six volumes of the " Letters and Journals " already published in Lord Ernle's Collected Edition of Byron's Works, in thirteen volumes (1898–1904).

Letters come into the market at uncertain periods, and cannot, therefore, be handled as a whole by the most judicious of editors. The letters in these somewhat belated volumes were originally the property of one of Byron's dearest friends and his executor, John Cam Hobhouse (" My Boy Hobbie O," in Volume VII. of the Poetry), afterwards Lord Broughton, and through him came into the possession of his daughter, Lady Dorchester, who in her turn bequeathed them to their present editor. The collection consists of some five hundred letters, chiefly of Byron's, though some from a diviner spirit, Shelley, illuminate the mass, and light up Byron's " tenement of clay."

Byron, in one respect at least, resembles Carlyle, for neither the one man nor the other ever wrote a letter that was not worth the trouble of printing. This unusual circumstance adds enormously to the task of the aforesaid " judicious editor," who, instead of being puzzled by the question, " Is this worth saving ? " asks himself, " How can I with-hold it ? " And yet a selection must be made when dealing with such inveterate scribblers as were Byron and Carlyle.

Mr. Murray, indeed, tells us in his introductory note that most of Byron's letters to his trustee, Mr. Douglas Kinnaird, have not been reprinted, as they consisted of " constantly repeated inquiries and instructions about investment of funds and other matters of no conceivable interest to any one now " ; but in the hands of a Byron or a Carlyle even often - repeated inquiries about " invest-ments " might have been made the vehicle of conveying the wildest strains of humour, and therefore of greater interest to the reader in 1922 than the unsavoury details of more important " matters."

Far too great a part of the first volume is taken up with an only too full and particular account of all that Byron endured during the years 1812 and

1813 from the mad vagaries of that wild melo-dramatic termagant, Lady Caroline Lamb.

Indeed, this whole story, already staled by frequent repetitions, would be quite unbearable were it not for one strange and mitigating circumstance, namely, that it is narrated to us, bit by bit, scene after scene, in a long series of letters, almost daily letters, written by Byron to Lady Caroline Lamb's mother-in-law, Lady Melbourne, the mother of William Lamb, the unlucky and long-suffering husband of the unfortunate Caroline. By a fortunate coincidence, Byron was immensely attracted by Lady Melbourne, who had more influence over his wayward nature than any other woman, and had she been but a little younger he must of necessity have fallen in love with her. Consequently these eternal letters, harping though they all do on this one screeching string, are, after a strange fashion of their own, at least half love-letters, and the tender feeling that runs through them makes their perusal, despite their theme, quite possible.

As for Lady Caroline herself, Byron's emotions towards her strangely fluctuate from a savage hatred to a still lingering attachment. Thus in this first volume he may be found writing :

The detestation, the bitter abhorrence I feel at part of the conduct I will neither shock you with nor trust myself to express. That feeling has become part of my nature ; it has poisoned my future existence. I know not whom I may love, but to the latest hour of my life I shall hate that woman. Now you know my sentiments—they will be the same on my death-bed. To her I do not express this, because I have no desire to make her uncomfortable, but such is the state of my mind towards her for reasons I shall not recur to. I beg to be spared from meeting her until we may be chained together in Dante's Inferno.

Yet when this detestable lady is at sea and tossing on the waves, Byron, instead of exultation, exhibits a certain tenderness towards her.

All readers of the first volume will agree that we really can have too much even of a bad thing, and I am not surprised to find the editor admitting that, if he had been allowed his own way, he would have made considerable omissions from " these rather wearisome iterations of the same theme." But he goes on to tell us that, as Lord Byron's " descendants have expressed a definite wish that all these letters to Lady Melbourne should be published *verbatim et literatim*," he had no choice in the matter. I must say, upon reading the letters all through, this decision comes very hard upon the " descendants " of other people. And all the time you cannot keep your thoughts away from the husband of this victim of vanity and hysteria. The future Prime Minister's forbearance almost exceeds belief ; but it seems true that the pair, but

for the unfortunate delusion about Byron, might
have been fairly happy together had it not been
that from the very first they made the initial mistake of assuming that married life may be treated
as a great joke, which it never can be. Lord Melbourne, indeed, might have been able to make a
joke out of life, either married or single, but for
his unlucky spouse it proved an impossibility.

Lady Caroline survived the man she tortured.

Judge what my horror was, as well as grief, when the news
came of his death ; it was conveyed to me in two or three
words, " Caroline, behave properly. I know it will shock you.
Lord Byron is dead." This letter came when I was laughing
at Brocket Hall. Its effect produced a fever from which I
have never yet recovered. It was also singular that the first
day I could go out in an open carriage, as I was very slowly
driving up the hill here, Lord Byron's hearse was at the moment
passing under these very walls, and rested at Welwyn. William
Lamb, who was riding on before me, met the procession at the
turnpike, and asked whose funeral it was. He was very much
affected and shocked—I, of course, was not told ; but as I kept
continually asking where and when he was to be buried, and
had read in the papers it was to be at Westminster Abbey, I
heard it too soon, and it made me very ill again. (" Letters and
Journals," Vol. II.)

Thus ends a distressful story.

The remainder of this first volume is concerned
with another almost equally painful and well-worn
tale, the wooing of Miss Milbanke, that " Princess
of Parallelograms," as her husband calls her. The
only real pleasure this marriage gave Byron was

that it enabled him, in his correspondence with Lady Melbourne, to call her " Aunt."

SEAHAM, *Feb.* 2, 1815.

MY DEAR AUNT,— . . . The *moon* is over; but Bell and I as lunatic as heretofore. She does as she likes, and don't bore me ; and we may win the Dunmow flitch of bacon for all I know. Mamma and Sir Ralph are also very good, but I wish the last would not speak his speech at the Durham meeting above once a week after its first delivery. . . .

Ever yours, most Nepotically,

B.

The second volume of this new correspondence is, happily for the general reader, of a more varied nature, and though of necessity it is concerned with a melancholy period of Byron's always troubled existence—his exile from England and his manner of life in Venice and Ravenna, and his death in Greece—the letters it makes known to us for the first time are full of that *élan*, that vivacity of expression, that audacious humour, often tinged with brutality, of those spontaneous and apt quotations, bespeaking not only familiarity with, but intense enjoyment of, his favourite old-fashioned authors, which place " Byron's Letters " amongst the most agreeable of literary experiences.

To give quotations is unnecessary, and might mislead the uninitiated. Byron was as strange a compound as ever came into this world. After reading these two volumes and refreshing my

memory of the former six, I am disposed to pro-
nounce Byron a good-tempered man. He was
called upon to endure much, not only from his
enemies, but from his friends. Hobhouse, for
example, was one of his best and oldest friends,
and yet how Byron was treated by him! There
was Byron all this time producing most magnificent poetry—" Childe Harold," " Don Juan,"
" The Vision of Judgment," etc.—and what has
Hobhouse to say to it ? Inept, foolish, peddling
criticism is all that Byron got in exchange for his
flattery of Hobhouse's mob-oratory and tenth-rate
publications. Then there were the dilatory law
agents, the difficulties over the sale of Newstead
and Rochdale, the Lady Caroline scandal, and a
hundred other things to pester and annoy. On the
whole, Byron kept his temper very well with
everybody save " Bob Southey."

I have already said that this second volume is
illuminated by long and hitherto unpublished
letters from Shelley. They are far too long for
quotation and too closely knit to be abridged. No
one should miss them. St. Francis never preached
more beautiful sermons.

As a critic of Byron's poetry—and these letters
contain many specimens of this criticism—Shelley

is excellent, particularly in what he has to say about " Don Juan."

We know what Shelley thought about Byron. What did Byron think about Shelley ? What a strange pair of immortals to be harnessed together even for a short time ! Trelawny's account of them both will always be on the top of our minds. There is no getting away from it. Trelawny knew them. We did not. Still, we must " allow for the wind," and Trelawny, who was a very " gusty " person, is not to be taken too literally. He had a certain jealousy of Byron that at times makes him unjust.

Shelley's behaviour to Allegra—Byron's daughter by Jane Clairmont—comes almost too near divinity to bear writing about. He and Mary Shelley bore the brunt, and endured the scandal. In this second volume may be read all about their conduct, and it imparts a halo to a book which often stands sorely in need of such an adornment.

In justice to Byron one other point must be made. Readers of Professor Dowden's " Life of Shelley " (two volumes, 1896) are not likely to forget the disgust and indignation raised in their minds against Byron when told that he had deliberately kept back and retained in his possession

until his death a long letter from Mrs. Shelley sent
to him to be forwarded to Mrs. Hoppner, the wife
of the British Consul in Venice, vindicating herself
and her husband from the odious charges brought
against them by Mr. Hoppner in a letter addressed
to Byron in September, 1820. Hoppner's letter
and Byron's shabby reply to it are to be found in
the second volume.

Hoppner's scandal was that, after the birth of
Allegra, Jane Clairmont had another child by
Shelley, which, immediately after its birth, had
been taken to the Pieta and the doctor's silence
secured by a bribe. These lies were told by a
former nurse to Allegra, one Elise Foggi, who
subsequently retracted them in writing.

In August, 1821, Shelley paid Byron a visit at
Ravenna, and in the course of conversation during
the first night of the meeting Byron showed
Shelley Hoppner's letter, then eleven months old.

Shelley thereupon wrote to his wife a letter
printed in this volume, and on receipt of this
letter Mary Shelley wrote the long letter to Mrs.
Hoppner now printed for the first time *in extenso*,
and sent it unsealed to Shelley at Ravenna, with
a request that he would read it to Lord Byron. It
was so read, and then sealed by Shelley and given

to Byron to be forwarded. This is the letter the original of which, after Byron's death, found its way into the Dorchester Collection with Shelley's seal broken.

Professor Dowden, on these facts, comes to the conclusion that Mary Shelley's letter, parts of which he prints from a copy which had somehow come into his possession, was deliberately retained by Byron, and never reached Mrs. Hoppner at all. Were this true, a baser act can hardly be imagined. But why believe it ? Byron may have sent the letter to the Hoppners under a separate cover and asked for its return. He was a sensible man, and to request its return would have been a sensible request. The Shelleys, who were not likely to rest until they knew the lie had been refuted, were satisfied, and the two poets remained on terms of affection till Shelley's death, when it was found he had named Byron one of his executors, and left him a legacy of £2,000, which Byron, though greedy of money, refused to take out of regard for the widow's poor circumstances.*

With these two volumes Byron's works, both poetry and prose (the famous " Memoirs " being

---

* As a matter of fact this legacy was not payable until after the death of Shelley's father, who survived Byron—but the generous intent was the same.

destroyed), may now for all literary purposes be declared complete. There they are, and there they will remain. Like Gibbon's "History," they will always be read both at home and abroad. Anxiety about Byron's vitality is quite out of place. His character and his rhythm, his morals and his grammar, will continue to be criticised, but he himself will always be alive.

The present editor somewhat pontifically assures us in his introduction that he has had better opportunities than most people of forming an opinion as to the position Byron holds in the public estimate, and that consequently he is in a position to inform the detractors of Byron's fame that their view is a false one.

The opinions of publishers as to their own wares is always a little " suspect " ; but Byron has long since escaped from the bondage of Albemarle Street and " overflowed the world."

Like Milton's Leviathan,

> Which God, of all His works,
> Created hugest,

he lies

> On the deep
> Stretched like a Promontory.

And there, in his own bad grammar, " let him lay."

IX.

THE GRENVILLE BROTHERS.*

(1920.)

It is, though this perhaps is putting it rather high, always pleasantly agreeable to read about the Grenville Brotherhood ; and this is particularly so when the medium of communication is the pen of one of the females of the family.

Of the Grenvilles it has been written :

> All men are brethren, bound to love each other !
> Gods ! how each Grenville loved his Grenville brother ;

and if by love is meant an ever-abiding desire to see every Grenville, in his turn, placed upon the Votes, the truth of Lord Lytton's couplet cannot be denied.

Half a century ago men took greater pleasure than they now appear to do in counting up the cost to the country of great families and highly-placed officials. When I was young, the " Liverpool Financial Reform Almanac " had a great local

---

* " Correspondence of Charlotte Grenville, Lady Williams Wynn, and her Three Sons (1795–1832)." Edited by Rachel Leighton. With illustrations. (Murray. 21s. net.)

vogue, and was the favourite reading of the budding Lancashire Radical, who could be relied upon
to tell you almost to a penny how much Lord
Thurlow's relatives had taken out of the Exchequer in costly sinecures. The Grenville
Brotherhood did not escape—how could they ?—
the lash of the reformer's whip ; nor is there anything in this family correspondence to turn aside
the application of the scourge. Little " Tom "
Grenville, the best of the whole batch, was, on the
completion of his fourth year, in the running for
the reversion of a clerkship in his uncle's office, and
merely to place on record the well-paid offices the
brethren held during a period of sixty years would
be a task demanding a far ampler reward than
could be hoped for in these days, when the interest
in such themes has notably slackened.

The truth is that the horrors of the present
moment, to say nothing of grim forebodings as to
the immediate future, seem to have taken away
our appetite for gloating over the financial excesses
of the past ; and as we cannot honestly affirm that
the age of gigantic jobbery is over, or that the
Thurlows and Grenvilles were not, taken as a
whole, as competent and industrious, and, at least,
as generally intelligent, as any State officials we are

ever likely to lay hands on, we are well content to
forget all about their nepotism and family greed.
Why, even that unlucky politician, George Grenville, the father of the lady whose letters to her
three sons are here exposed, though assuredly no
genius, could, if Dr. Johnson may be credited,
count upon his fingers up to ten, and would therefore have made to-day as good a Minister as—
well, as anybody !

To describe the ramifications of the Grenville
pedigree would be a task both " rash and ridiculous," and, in the words of Tom Hood, would

> Puzzle Old Nick,
> Not to name Sir Harris Nicholas,

but, fortunately for the enjoyment of these letters,
it is only necessary to grasp the fact that the
mother of this particular brood was a daughter of
George Grenville of " Stamp Act " notoriety, by
his happy union with a daughter of the more
famous Sir William Wyndham, the Jacobite friend
of Bolingbroke and Swift. This Mrs. Grenville
died in 1769, leaving seven children behind, including another George Grenville, who became
Earl Temple and, in due Grenvillian course, Mar-
quis of Buckingham ; and a William Wyndham
Grenville, who, after filling numerous offices, such

as Chief Secretary to the Lord Lieutenant of Ireland and Speaker of the House of Commons, became, in 1806, a Prime Minister as head of the short-lived Administration known as " All the Talents " ; and a third son, Thomas, who, though tainted with the family malady, for he long held a sinecure office of £2,000 a year, as well as being President of the Board of Control and, afterwards, First Lord of the Admiralty, in his brother's Cabinet, still smells sweet and blossoms in the dust of the British Museum, where slumber the 20,000 rare books, purchased no doubt with public plunder, but which, by the terms of what the Romans called a pious will, were restored to their true owners, who still possess, even if they do not daily read, " Uncle Tom's " rarities.

One " Uncle Tom " in a family goes far as a fertiliser of the soil, for we find one of his nephews, aged fourteen, writing to another nephew in 1796 as follows :

STOWE, *Friday*, 1796.

I have had a great many books given me lately. Lord Howard (de Walden) sent me a very fine set of Harding's Plates to Johnson and Steven's " Shakespeare." Mr. Gretton gave me a nice Baskerville Milton. Uncle Buckingham gave a very curious book called " Breydenbach's Peregrination " ; it was printed in 1486, and was the first book of Voyages ever printed. Lord Temple gave me Gibbon's " Roman Empire," 12 volumes octavo, Clarendon's " History of the Rebellion," and Lucretius Catullus and Virgil, printed by Baskerville. Uncle Grenville (not " Tom," but the Prime Minister that was to be) also gave me a Molière, 6 volumes quarto ;

and in another letter the same boy, writing this time from Eton, adds :

I have got all my books here, and am going to have a new bookcase, not having half room. Are you all books at Harrow ? I forgot to ask to see your bookcase when I was at Taplow.

These are remarkable letters for a small Etonian to write to a cousin of his own age. And what delightful books !

This small boy lived to become the third Lord Braybrooke and editor of the *Editio princeps* of Pepy's Diary in five handsome volumes. Lord Braybrooke did not himself decipher and transcribe Pepys' shorthand, for that " task " was " allotted " to a humble curate of the name of John Smith, with whom his lordship " was not personally acquainted." *

I must return to less exciting topics. Charlotte Grenville, Lady Williams Wynn married a year after her father's death the fourth baronet of the well-known Welsh line, and after Sir Watkin's death in 1789 became, under the terms of his will, sole trustee of his great estates, and sole executrix and guardian of his six children, then all infants.

* John Smith's task was not a very difficult one, for a key to the cipher was with the papers all the time.

Sir Watkin's confidence was not misplaced, for, as this correspondence reveals, his widow possessed to a remarkable degree what men call a " masculine " intelligence, that assumed, without a moment's doubt or demur, the full responsibilities of her position. Her children, boys and girls alike, all dutifully acknowledged her ability and returned her affection, and allowed her to the end of her days to play the wise and authoritative matronal *rôle*. She corrects their spelling, criticises their modes of expression, deplores, in the case of her sons, their supineness in the chase of eligible, if ugly, heiresses, and generally instructs them in the ways a Grenville mother would naturally wish her children to go, and this she did for more than forty years without ever trying her children's tempers or lessening their affection.

It is this firm yet friendly family relationship that gives this correspondence so agreeable a tone, for otherwise the volume itself cannot be described as either particularly edifying or very amusing.

Of the three sons on whom this mother bestowed her energy and worldly wisdom the eldest, Watkin, embraced arms as his profession, and it was his fortune to flesh his maiden sword in the Irish

Rebellion of 1798, and to be present in command of his company of " Ancient British Dragoons " at the glorious engagement of Vinegar Hill.

Irish " extracts " are always painful reading, and apparently unprofitable, for nobody is ever mended by them. The youthful Sir Watkin writes on July 13th, 1798 :

> As my regiment was idle, I was for the last four days as a volunteer with General Lake hunting after the Rebels through the mountains of Wicklow, but unluckily we could not catch them, they are gone North of Dublin, where they have had a good dressing, and are attacked on all sides. Now that they are driven out of the mountains they cannot long exist.

Possibly not, but their descendants exist one hundred and twenty years afterwards.

Semper eadem is the maxim for English rule in Ireland. Lord Cornwallis, that much experienced man in all parts of the Empire, failed, so we here read, by his excessive lenity to the rank and file of the rebels and his arbitrary treatment of their leaders, " the result being that his acts of leniency were misinterpreted as weakness, and his attitude towards the leaders regarded as cruel and vindictive."

Another extract :

> By the autumn of 1798 the Rebellion had ceased ; all that remained was smouldering hatred and distrust, on which was built up the fabric of the United Parliament of 1800.

I hope the new Irish Parliaments will be found to
have better foundations.

But Ireland has never lacked really wise and
far-seeing advisers. Sir Watkin met one of these
gentry in Dublin, who bore the " John Bunyan "
name of " Ogle." Mr. Ogle assured the young
soldier " that he firmly believed this rebellion
could *never* be extinguished but by the revival of
the penal statutes against the Catholics, the laying
waste with fire and sword any district in which the
rebels should continue in force, and the complete
extermination of every person who ever joined the
standard of rebellion." The race of " Ogle " has
never been " exterminated," and to-day flourishes
side by side with the " unextinguished " Rebellion
of 1798, and the new Parliaments of 1920.

Sir Watkin, after his return from the hunting in
the Wicklow mountains, settled down on his
family estate, sat for Denbighshire in the House of
Commons, and, wanting nothing, was apparently
content, although a Grenville, to ask for nothing.
At all events, he got nothing.

Charles, the second son, had a different kind of
life, and was always on the lookout for anything
" suitable." He was a barrister, but did not
practise in the courts of law. He sat in Parlia-

ment for " his own county of Montgomery " con-
tinuously for fifty years. He was once a candidate
for the Speakership, but a too obvious, and therefore a good, House of Commons joke spoilt his
chance. His voice was not deep, and there were
parliamentarians who dreaded that some unruly
and possibly inebriate Member, on being called to
order, might, either wilfully or through thickness
of utterance, refer to the occupant of the chair as
" Mr. Squeaker." Charles and his mother felt this
untoward rebuff very keenly, and though Charles
is reported to have three times refused the
Governor-Generalship of India, and certainly held,
for one year, the Chancellorship of the Duchy of
Lancaster, he died unconsoled in 1850.

Henry, the youngest son, who was only seven at
his father's death, was always his mother's darling.
He had what is called " a taste for travel," filled
various diplomatic appointments, visited the Holy
Land, and collected books for " Uncle Tom." He
was the most affectionate of all the family.

The correspondence is full of marriages,
divorces, match - makings in high life, and of
scandalous, unkind, and acidulated observations
upon half the old peerage. The new peers may
find these parts amusing.

X.

THE GODS OF YESTERDAY.*

(1918.)

THIS is a delightful book, full of the best qualities of authorship, and, having the charm and all the authority of youth, it is sure to travel far and make many friends. One of its qualities is the pleasure-giving quality, and in many, though not perhaps in all, quarters " Eminent Victorians " will be read and re-read with pleasure and with profit. Elderly folk who are beginning to move slowly about the ground, with figures " grown convex," may find in its pages just a little too much, despite the prevailing note of a dexterous urbanity, of that unkindness of judgment which is characteristic of critics who have not yet been judged by their juniors. Reason, as was shrewdly said by a great scholar of our own day, is the philosophy which is in vogue for the moment, and,

* " Eminent Victorians : Manning, Florence Nightingale, Dr. Arnold, General Gordon." By Lytton Strachey. (Chatto and Windus).

as such philosophies are of necessity shortlived, even the test of Reason should be applied cautiously, and possibly humbly, to the lives and creeds of our predecessors.

With this *caveat*, demanded by the birthdays which lie behind me, I return thanks for this book of Mr. Strachey, which may confidently be recommended to all would-be biographers. In the short but valuable Preface the author speaks, almost bitterly, of too many modern biographies :

> Those two fat volumes with which it is our custom to commemorate the dead—who does not know them, with their ill-digested masses of material, their slipshod style, their tone of tedious panegyric, their lamentable lack of selection, of detachment, of design ? They are as familiar as the *cortège* of the undertaker, and wear the same air of slow, funereal barbarism. One is tempted to suppose of some of them that they were composed by that functionary as the final item of his job.

Know them indeed ! " Who knows them if not I ? " Without having at this moment any particular specimen in my mind, I can never think of this class of " Standardised Biography " without something between a shudder and a groan. Oh, those familiar headings ! " Birth and Parentage," " School Days," " The University," " Early Struggles," " Choice of a Profession," " Marriage," " Foreign Travel," and so on, through the dull, devitalising record, until your tired eye rests with an unbecoming joy upon the familiar words " Ill-Health, Death, and Characteristics." Such things promote blasphemy. Future biographers of modern celebrities will do well to keep these caustic pages of Mr. Strachey by their side as they write as a *memento mori*.

All this is by the way.

Mr. Strachey frankly explains his method. He is interested, as an outsider (for apparently he owns " another birth "), in the Victorian Age. He has read about it in hundreds of volumes. He loves details, and has the seeing eye and a most observant thumb. He would have written a history of it if he could, but the task is too huge. Oblivion, which alone makes wisdom possible, has not yet come to the relief of the historian of the Victorian Age, and so Mr. Strachey was driven to other courses :

Concerning the age which has just passed, our fathers and grandfathers have poured forth and accumulated so vast a quantity of information that the industry of a Ranke would be submerged by it, and the perspicuity of a Gibbon would quail before it. It is not by the direct method of scrupulous narration that the explorer of the past can hope to depict that singular epoch. If he is wise he will adopt a subtler strategy. He will attack his subject in unexpected places, he will fall upon the flank or the rear ; he will shoot a sudden, revealing searchlight into obscure recesses. He will row out over that great ocean of material and lower down into it, here and there, a little bucket, which will bring up to the light of day some character-

istic specimen from those far depths to be examined with
a careful curiosity. Guided by these considerations, I have
written the ensuing studies. I have attempted through the
medium of biography to present some Victorian visions to the
modern eye. They are in some sense haphazard visions—that
is to say, my choice of subjects has been determined by no
desire to construct a system or to form a theory, but by simple
motives of convenience and art.

Notwithstanding this honest avowal of " simple
motives," an old man easily perceives that this
means mischief. A " subtle strategy," even if
conducted only by searchlights and a little bucket,
could hardly fail to bring to the surface some
things belonging to that " singular epoch " which
to the " modern eye " must seem almost im-
possibly odd and even absurd.

And here one is forced to ask, How did Mr.
Strachey select his menagerie, his caged animals,
whom he attacks upon the flank or the rear, sometimes shooting searchlights into their obscure
recesses, and sometimes squirting his ironical
humour over them through the bars ? It is indeed
an interesting method, entirely jumping with the
humour of the day ; nor does it raise any question
of actual unkindness, for do we not all know very
well that Mr. Strachey's cages are empty ? There
is nobody there to be wounded or hurt ; only at
the most, littered in the corners, small fragments

of biography, letters, and the like, from which the
onlooker, if he has enough imagination, can recon-
struct for himself the deserted lairs, the beds on
which, during that "singular epoch," wounded
human spirits turned in their pain and irresolution
—just as living human beings are doing to-day.
Mr. Strachey tells us that he chose his victims by
the simple method of convenience and art, and I
must therefore assume that it is an artistic sense
of unity that has led the author in this, his first
gallery of portraits, to include no one who could,
in any true sense of the word, be called a
Rationalist. In his next strategical movement
Mr. Strachey will, I hope, attack, let me suggest
among others, John Mill, James Martineau, and
Mark Pattison. This is almost necessary to
balance his boat.

All Mr. Strachey's studies are so fascinating and
artistically handled that to describe them, save by
long quotations, would be impossible; and to
quote would be to destroy the pleasure of the
reader when he takes up the book for himself.
There is, however, one of them which, personally,
I could wish away. It seems to me that Dr.
Arnold of Rugby is a little out of place in this
highly-finished and ironical gallery of portraits.

G 2

Arnold was a very good man, and, once upon a time, what is lightly called a great man ; but he has long disappeared, save in the harmless and now fading tradition of a book for boys, " Tom Brown's Schooldays," and in a noble, filially inspired poem, " Rugby Chapel."

It is, I know, always dangerous to assert positively of a once-popular author that nobody reads him ; but this I can say, that for many years I have sought in vain for any one *who, born after January 1st*, 1865, had read even one of Dr. Arnold's seventeen volumes or his " Life," by Dean Stanley, much bepraised as that biography has always been. In Mr. Strachey, it appears, I have at last met my man.

It so happened that just before " Eminent Victorians " came my way I was re-reading, and not even for the second time, a review, once famous in certain circles, of Stanley's famous biography by no less renowned a thinker than Dr. Martineau. This review first appeared in 1845, a year after the biography, and this, I suppose, in Mr. Strachey's opinion, is a very long time ago. So it may be, but for all that, when I came to behold in " Eminent Victorians " the vision of Dr. Arnold, I was almost startled to notice how, all unconsciously, the critic of to-day had taken, in all essentials, the same point of view (however differently expressed) as had been taken more than seventy years ago by the Arian divine. The two critics had marked the same passages for animadversion upon, or elucidation of, Arnold's character. This concurrence, though startling, was not really surprising, for Dr. Arnold was from the very beginning exceedingly obvious to any " unblinkered " observer, Christian or otherwise.

Arnold's influence, and for a short time it was great, was wholly personal. Martineau, in his review (which may be found in his " Miscellanies," 1852, and I dare say elsewhere), writes of him as " respectable in scholarship, insensible to art, undistinguished in philosophy, great in action, though his sphere was not large." He disliked science, yet was no theologian, save on the ethical side, and, notwithstanding his enormous activity in writing, he was never at any time taken as a leader of thought, or even of opinion. His was a boyish intelligence. Mr. Strachey's observant eye has noticed, from a portrait, that there was always " a slightly puzzled look upon Dr. Arnold's face," and, indeed, he was easily puzzled. The parentage of Abijah's mother puzzled him. The authorship of the Epistle to the Hebrews puzzled him. Whether Unitarians could be called Christians puzzled him (Dr. Newman, *per contra*, though he loved the man, had no doubt that Arnold, at all events, was not a Christian); but the greatest source of Arnold's puzzlement was that, though he *saw*, with his ethical clear-sightedness, that England was not a Christian country and had a non-Christian Government, yet he was forced by his ecclesiastical theories to *believe* that it was one, or, by simple constitutional changes, might easily be turned into one. Such a man, so simple, so straightforward, so entirely ethical, is, I think, though I daresay I am wrong, out of place in this highly specialised volume ; but if Mr. Strachey were to say that his book is called "Eminent Victorians," and Dr. Arnold was for a while an eminent Victorian, it might be hard to find an answer.

If a doubt may be entertained as to the insertion of this vision of Dr. Arnold, there can be none that in the two cardinals, Manning and Newman, Mr. Strachey has found subjects made to his hand. Newman is not indeed named in the list of contents, but, for all that, his portrait is to be seen hanging, *vis-a-vis* to Manning's, in this gallery.

How much reading, reflection, and perception has gone to produce these two pictures no one who has not traversed the same paths of study can form any adequate idea. These one hundred and fourteen pages are at once criticism and drama. Perhaps the drama here prevails a little over the criticism. Mr. Strachey's visualisation of his figures is so intense that he is led to compare Manning to an eagle, and Newman to a dove. " It was the meeting of the eagle and the dove ; there was a hovering and a swoop, and then the quick beak and the relentless talons did their work " (p. 76). Any one less like a dove than J. H. N. it would be hard to picture. We are, indeed, told by ornithologists that doves are quarrelsome birds, but they are not fierce, and yet we know from Newman's own honest con- fession, and also *aliunde*, that throughout his whole life he had to contend against a certain fierceness of temper which made him defiant in word and deed. And as for the eagle, Bossuet has earned that sobriquet, but hardly Manning, of whom a clerical brother-in-law unkindly said that the seeming magnificence of his forehead was attributable to the fact that he had no face.

Mr. Strachey may safely be relied upon to bring out in high relief the contrast between these two

men, and to give full dramatic effect to their unfortunate encounters.   It is a violent contrast, and
the encounters are so disagreeable that one can
surely wish, without being thought vaporish or
sentimental, that Mr. Purcell had not supplied us
with such ample materials for making the contrast
and for moralising on the encounters.

Mr. Strachey, in his Biography, does not mention as one of his " sources " Francis Newman's
amazing memoranda about his big brother.   Never
were two good men, and naturally affectionate
brothers, so hopelessly at arm's-length from the
very first.   Francis was always nervously on the
look-out to find a common topic about which he
could confidently approach " My dear John " ;
and on one luckless occasion, after listening to a
" magnificent " speech to a " rapt " audience in
the Free Trade Hall, Manchester, from Manning
on Temperance, he thought he had found one.   He
sat down and, with his heart full of elation and
joy, he told his brother in glowing language all
about the Archbishop of Westminster's great
triumph.   " He replied in a kind note, but with
only these few words bearing on my topic : ' As
to what you tell me of Archbishop Manning, I have
heard that some also of our Irish bishops think

that too many drinkshops are licensed. As for me, I do not know whether we have too many or too few.' " Francis adds : " This seemed to curdle my heart like a lump of ice " ; and so down he sat again and composed, as if coming from J. H. N., " an imaginary reply " of quite another character than the real one, which concluded thus : " Be sure that you all, and the Archbishop, carry my heart warmly with your joint efforts " (" The Early History of Cardinal Newman." By his Brother. Kegan Paul, 1891.)

My sympathy with Francis would be even greater than it is were I quite sure there was not just a tinge of malice in his enthusiasm about the Archbishop in a letter to the Oratorian.

The vision of Florence Nightingale is a spirited and even magnificent bit of writing, whilst the story of General Gordon, with its searching lights upon the " obscure recesses " of the characters of Lord Cromer, Lord Hartington, and Mr. Gladstone holds you in its grip from first to last.

This is an unconventional volume, but I will part with it conventionally by saying that it is one you lay down with regret and will take up again with pleasure.

XI.

THE REACTIONARY WRITERS.*

(1903.)

In the strange, eventful history of human thought and endeavour, which for ever sounds in the ear like the distant roar of ocean, few chapters are fuller of melancholy and discomfiture than those which narrate to us who still stand " on the naked shingles of the world " the history of the inevitable reaction of men's minds against opinions which once possessed them with uncritical, and therefore unreal, violence. It is not a cheerful sight to witness this sudden reversal of thought, and to see men going back upon themselves and reverting, though with changed outlook and very different dispositions, to what had but a short while before seemed disposed of for ever. A reader may be fully alive to the weaknesses of Rousseau and yet find it hard to stifle a sigh as he lays down

* " Main Currents in Nineteenth Century Literature." By George Brandes. Six vols. Vol. III. (London : Wm. Heinemann, 1903. 9s. net.)

that moving writer and takes up De Maistre. Who
would not believe, if he could, that the world which
lies before us

> Like a land of dreams
> So various, so beautiful, so new,

has really hidden in her future, not only " joy and
love," but " light and certitude," or, if not these
fine things, at least some release from those perpetual doubts which De Tocqueville in his maturity
declared to be the most insupportable of all evils ?
Yet if we are to be for ever bandied about from one
extreme to another, now boasting our reason and
bragging about the natural sciences, and then,
sickened by our own verbosity and conceit, re-
mumbling ancient *credos* and paradoxically main-
taining old formulas, it is hard to resist the
conclusion of the poet just quoted :

> That we are here as on a darkling plain
> Swept with confused alarms of struggle and fight,
> Where ignorant armies clash by night.

George Brandes, indeed, has a confident spirit,
and, after tracing the history of the reaction in
France down to the dissolution of the school of
authority, he brings the volume to an abrupt close
with the exclamation, " And the principle falls,
never to rise again ! " But who knows ? *Che
sara, sara.*

The history of authority is a long one, and admits of being written from different points of view, but in the France of the eighteenth century authority had become personified in the Church, who presided over it and ladled it out as it was wanted to keep society as then constituted a going concern. To kings it granted divine right, and to peoples the comforts of the Sacraments and of an infallible guide in matters of faith and doctrine. It was a working system so long as no questions were asked. But the critical spirit is a questioning spirit. The questions were asked and the system was shattered. Yet, when the Revolution began and the Estates assembled, the clergy flocked thither in good faith with their demand that the Catholic and Apostolic and Roman religion should be recognised as the national faith, with the exclusive monopoly of public worship. Later on, when the National Assembly was constituted, it took part in church processions and, in its public capacity, attended Mass. But the scene soon shifts to disclose horrors. The destruction of Christianity was, on the face of things, complete, and Dr. Brandes reminds us that the hatred of priests and the fierce determination that France should never again be at their feet was of long duration. The iconoclasm was carried out with French thoroughness. But for all that it was a failure. Our author says :

The men of the Revolution had failed to comprehend that the great body of the people, profoundly ignorant and imbued with ideas and feelings which had been transmitted from generation to generation for centuries, were irresponsive to their appeals, terrified by their acts of violence, and prepared from old habit to give themselves over into the hands of the priests again as soon as opportunity offered. In 1800, in a letter to Bonaparte, General Clarke writes : " Our religious revolution has been a failure, France has become Roman Catholic again. It would take thirty years' liberty of the Press to destroy the spiritual power of the Bishop of Rome." He is mistaken only in his computation of thirty years. Three hundred would be more nearly the number required.

Before the Concordat with the Pope of 1802 France had enjoyed, for a brief season it is true, complete religious liberty and the full swing of the voluntary system. The priests were supported wholly by their congregations, and every religious teacher enjoyed equally the protection of the law. Bonaparte had to choose between the principle of religious liberty and the sanction of the Church. " He did not," says M. Brandes, " deliberate long ; the re-establishment of the Church was an indispensable link in the chain of his policy."

Bonaparte had no religion in his system, and frankly avowed that he regarded the Concordat " as the inoculation of the State against religion,"

but what was he to do ? He required for himself
and his house the sanction of religion. He was
himself afraid of the questioning spirit, therefore
he kidnapped the Pope and, under duress, extorted
a blessing. Protestantism would not serve his
turn. " The principal charm of a religion," quoth
this prince of sentimentalists, " lies in its
memories. When I am at Malmaison I never
hear the church bell of the neighbouring village
ring without feeling moved. And in France who
could feel moved in a Protestant church ? "

But behind the statecraft of Bonaparte and the
rooted habits of the French peasant was a genuine
thought movement, begotten by the time-spirit
which worked independently of the First Consul
and Emperor, and soon developed a deadly hos-
tility to him, and openly declared itself on the
side of Pope and Bourbon. It is with this thought-
movement that restored the French monarchy,
and found its chief literary expression in the
writings of Chateaubriand, De Maistre, and
Bonald, that this volume of Dr. Brandes' is
mainly concerned.

No one of the three remarkable men just named
was of deeply religious nature—they were not
fervent, devout spirits. Their work was more

political than religious. They regarded faith as the mortar which kept the bricks of society sticking together.

Chateaubriand made a great parade of Christianity, and served it up again and again in dishes which were found appetising, but he never more than half believed in God, and his taste for religion was in keeping with the voluptuous disposition of his mind and character. We, who have his Memoirs to instruct us, can easily recognise the manner of man he was—a dissatisfied egoist, a confirmed doubter, full of quick insight into character and the course of events, but without the power to grasp his fate in both hands ; a prey to ennui and disgust, full of the grandeur of God and King, but without a constant faith in the one and with a very real contempt for the other when taking the form of Louis XVIII. He yet fabled his times, and by his gift of high-sounding words and his shadowy creations, profoundly moved the minds of men and women in the direction of the Reaction.

Joseph De Maistre was a man of very different calibre. Though one of the most distinguished of French writers, he spent but a few days of his hard life on French soil. De Maistre abhorred the

Revolution and its begetters from the earliest be-
ginnings. He had never, as had Chateaubriand,
tampered with the accursed thing. Nothing would
content him but the solemn repudiation of every
belief, opinion, phrase, which had in any way
whatever contributed towards the intellectual
outfit of this hideous ebullition. He repeated, in
another sense, with a far fiercer determination,
Voltaire's *Écrasez l'infâme*. Without kings who
were absolute there could be no Government ;
without a Pope who was infallible there could be
no Christianity ; nobody but God could make
laws ; a written constitution was a blasphemous
absurdity, a republic an impossibility ; there
never could be a city called Washington, and, even
if there could be, Congress would never meet in it.
A Reactionist, indeed ! and a most charming
writer. The English reader will find in Sir James
Stephens's " Horæ Sabbaticæ " an admirable
analysis of De Maistre's opinions, and in Mr.
Morley's Miscellanies a delightful account of the
man and his books.

Dr. Brandes thus sums up De Maistre—a little
unkindly, but with essential truth :

His Christianity is an entirely external thing. He is a
Christian as a man is a Protectionist or a Free Trader, on
grounds of general theoretical conviction. His Christianity is a

Christianity without brotherly love—nay, it is a Christianity without Christ as a saviour and reconciler. In it Christ is only the sanguinary sacrifice demanded by the offended deity—like Iphigenia or Jepthah's daughter. Faquet has aptly said that De Maistre's Christianity is fear, passive obedience, and State religion. It is a Christianity which does not originate in Jerusalem, but in Rome, and he himself is something in the nature of an officer of the Pope's bodyguard.

In reactionary times * it is wise to study the history of a great reaction, and whoever reads this book of Dr. Brandes' will find much in it for sober reflection.

* When Mussolinis succeed Mazzinis.

XII.

APROPOS OF A BIOGRAPHY.*

(1898.)

BIOGRAPHIES abound.   Some think they may
come to threaten the supremacy of the novel.   A
paradoxical friend of our own has been heard to
asseverate that it is becoming daily harder to live
his own life, so crowded out has it become with the
details of the lives of other people.   The fact is
biography, and still more autobiography, jumps
with the humour of the time.   It is a sop thrown
to realism.   " You call my life dull, do you ? " the
autobiographer may exclaim ;   " but, anyhow, I
lived it."   Before the twentieth century breathes
its last the number of autobiographies in English
will have increased by leaps and bounds.   Why
not ?   As the poet sings :

> Lives of small men all remind us
>   Each should write his life himself,
> And departing leave behind him
>   Two octavos on the shelf.

For our part, we regard the huge impending

* " Sir Charles Murray, K.C.B." A Memoir. By Sir Herbert
Maxwell, M.P. (London: Blackwood & Co.)

output with what Dr. Johnson has called " a gigantic calm." There are very few really bad autobiographies. One of the best is Tupper's.

These observations, however valuable, have next to nothing to do with the biography before us. To call Sir Charles Murray a small man would be at least as absurd as to call him a great one. His was a distinguished and a romantic figure, whose life was far removed from the ordinary. It was well worth writing, and Sir Herbert Maxwell has written it with his accustomed deftness. The result is a book profitable to read and pleasant to keep. Murray was a Scot of ancient and well-accredited lineage and high spirits, and he added to these qualities, as his days grew, a fine sense of the gravity of life and the true scope of things. It is not surprising to learn that Wordsworth's poetry, though a little late, made a lively impression on his mind ; for Murray's mind was of the Wordsworthian order ; and what higher praise can be paid a man than to hold him akin to him from whom we may learn " to look on Nature with a humble heart " ? Had Murray known his Wordsworth earlier than appears to have been the case, he might have been saved the most unsatisfactory years of his life.

H 2

Scotch pedigrees are our pet aversion, but, unless we misunderstand the matter, Charles Augustus Murray, who was undoubtedly born in 1806, was a son of the fifth Earl of Dunmore in the Scottish peerage—the first Baron Dunmore of the United Kingdom—by his marriage with a daughter of the ninth Duke of Hamilton. Old Samuel Rogers was a friend of Lady Dunmore's, and quite a considerable number of his letters fill the early pages of this book. They are not as good as they ought to be. Lady Dunmore was an excellent woman—a pious woman—but we owe her a grudge that her correspondent was not Sydney Smith instead of Samuel Rogers. Murray spent his childhood in a romantic and solitary glen on the shores of Loch Long. In the year of Waterloo he was sent to Eton, whither he was accustomed to go, sometimes in rough weather *via* Norway, in a smack from Leith to London. In 1822 he left Eton and proceeded to a private tutor—the Vicar of Sunninghill—with whom he read two years. Then he went to Oxford. All that we are told either of Eton or Oxford as educational establishments is what we may learn from Murray's statement that it was to the vicar he owed " the strong love for the classics which he maintained through life."

Murray's college was Oriel, his tutor John Henry Newman. The very names, like church bells, seem to

> Make catholic the trembling air.

Oxford, Oriel, and Newman, the Wordsworthian mind of the youthful Murray, the fascination of the future cardinal — here surely are romance and mystery enough for one volume. Happy biographer ! But no ; here is nothing of the kind :

> Newman never inspired me or my fellow-undergraduates with any interest, much less respect ; on the contrary, we disliked, or, rather distrusted, him. He walked with his head bent, abstracted, but every now and then looking out of the corners of his eyes quickly, as though suspicious. . . . At lectures he was quiet, and what I should call sheepish—stuck to his text and never diverged into contemporary history or made the lecture interesting. He always struck me as the most pusillanimous of men, wanting in the knowledge of human nature. . . . I never heard him preach.

Then follows the story of the bell-rope. Sir Herbert Maxwell's observation that Newman's " gentle, thoughtful mind failed to secure the affection of those terrible youngsters " is more amiable than adequate. There was nothing " gentle " about Newman's mind. His manners may have been gentle, or, at least, subdued ; but his mind and temper were both fierce, nor did the lapse of more than half a century or the religious repose of

the Oratory subdue his native fire, or dispose him
to submit to misrepresentation at the hands,
grown aged, of " the high and mighty youths who,
relying on the claims of family and fortune, did
their best to oppose me and spread tales about
me." That Newman's ironic and sarcastic
methods were lost upon the noisiest of his pupils
is like enough, nor can any reader of his brother's
amazing little pamphlet be blind to the fact that
J. H. N. had a repellent, almost a repulsive, side
to his character. But pusillanimity! the notion
of his being afraid to face half a handful of rowdy
boys " swoln with insolence and wine "!—these
are ideas not now to be entertained.

It is melancholy to have to note of so fine a
fellow as Murray that the place where all that was
good in him had the least chance was Oxford. He
took a pass degree and " formed the ambition to
be elected a Fellow of All Souls." Why ambition?
Design would surely be the better word, for he does
not seem to have passed any examination. His
pedigree, his tailor, and his high spirits were his
passports to the Fellows' table. He then began to
consider a profession—or, rather, his mother seems
to have done so on his behalf. In 1828 Brougham
inflicted upon Lady Dunmore the long letter he

was in the habit of despatching to those of his
friends who had sons thinking of the Bar or
Parliament. It is chiefly about Demosthenes—
" If he would be a great orator he must at once go
to the fountain-head and be familiar with every
one of the great orations of Demosthenes, for I
take it for granted he knows those of Cicero by
heart." The pity of it is none of the sons ever took
old Verbosity's advice to heart, and so we cannot
say what would have happened if they had.

It would be unfair to tell the romance of Sir
Charles Murray's life. Biographies have their
plots as well as novels. His travels among the
Pawnees—real Fenimore-Cooper Red Indians—
where, lying out during starry nights in the silent
prairies, he learnt more " of moral evil and of
good " than he had done at Oriel and All Souls ;
his life in the Court of the young Queen, his diplomatic adventures, his marriages, his religious
opinions, all these must be looked for in the book
itself.

No biography is complete unless it has at least
one story which is both good and new. This
biography contains one story about Lord Eldon
which is both. " Sitting opposite to Lord Eldon
one night at Hamilton Palace and fixing his eye

on the great lawyer, Hamilton of Dalzell suddenly
asked him, ' Have you ever read Dr. Spurzheim's
two great volumes on phrenology ? ' ' No, sir,'
replied Lord Eldon, ' and I'd be ashamed to own
it if I had.' "

XIII.

HENRY FIELDING AND THE LITERARY TRADITION.*

(1919.)

IT would indeed be an agreeable thing, were it possible, to take a leaf out of the book of the author of "A Journey from this World to the Next," and go in search of Henry Fielding, and to find him, perhaps, still playing with the little daughter he had lost years before his own departure, and formally to make a presentation to him of these three magnificent and well-illustrated volumes, the product of the boundless enthusiasm and unsleeping labour of an American editor, and of the resources of an American University Press, aided by the Foundation established in memory of an American lover of English letters.

If ever there lived a Man it was Henry Fielding, and, as he was also a writing man, we shall be safe in assuming, without crediting him with more than a double dose of vanity, that to handle even in

* "The History of Henry Fielding." By Wilbur L. Cross. Three Vols. (New Haven : Yale University Press. London : Milford. 63s. net.)

that " pensive place," the next world, this noble
biography—so happily entitled, after his own
manner, the " History of Henry Fielding "—could
not but afford the author of " The History of Tom
Jones " the most intense gratification.

And yet, though this, perhaps, is to be too
fanciful, could we by a further stroke of the
imagination, and after making our presentation,
pursue Fielding to a quiet corner, quite out of the
reach of Addison and Steele, and observe him as
he sat down and began to read this intensive
biography (containing, so Mr. Cross assures us,
almost as many words as " Tom Jones "), we should
be ready to swear, before Fielding's successor in
Bow Street, that we saw stealing across a coun-
tenance which, however etherealised, must still re-
tain its original Hogarthian air, a smile, magically
composed, in almost equal proportions, of surprise,
amusement, and of irony.

The last-mentioned quality belongs more naturally to this unintelligible world than to the next
one, which may possibly admit of explanation ;
but, as it would be impossible to picture an
unironical Fielding, we must be allowed, if we are
to suppose him smiling, to invest that expression
with at least a tincture of his greatest gift. But, it

may be asked, why should we suppose him to smile at all whilst engaged in reading his own Life?

Mr. Cross has flung himself so whole-heartedly into his work, and has done it so well, that it is an almost ungracious thing to begin finding fault with him from the very start ; but as the only complaint we have to make lies on the threshold of the subject, we may as well get rid of it at once, particularly as it may help to explain the imaginary smile.

Mr. Cross has found it necessary to quarrel with the great Fielding Tradition, which he would like to root up altogether and cast into the oven.

It is always dangerous to quarrel outright with Tradition. Be content with making ample allowances for mere gossip, for absurd exaggeration, for improper development, for spite and for malice ; but if, not content with this " toning-down," you go on to kick Tradition out of court altogether, and send her packing with a flea in her ear, what have you left, one hundred and sixty years afterwards, on which to build your characterisation ?

In the case of an author like Fielding you have his books, his plays, poems, novels. In the case of an orator you have (possibly) his speeches ; of a divine, his sermons ; of a philosopher, his treatises ; of a painter, his pictures ; of a table-talker, scraps of his conversation ; of a letter writer, his published correspondence ; and perchance there may be portraits by a Hogarth, a Reynolds, a Sargent, or a John. Aids to characterisation may be obtained from these quarters, and by the light thus thrown Tradition may, more or less confidently, be modified, corrected, contradicted, but never wholly superseded.

In Fielding's case we read his three famous novels, his glorious miscellanies, his comedies (if we can), his burlesques, and his last book of all, the " Journey to Lisbon," where he died in 1754, in his forty-eighth year. In these books he tells us much about himself. How could he help doing so ? As Bagehot says about Shakespeare, men do not keep tame steam engines to write their books for them. They write them themselves ; and there they remain on our shelves, in our hands bearing their testimony.

If the Fielding Tradition, as it has come down to us, gives the lie to the testimony of his books, the conflict would be serious ; but does it ?

The reader of the books must answer this question for himself, and, if he is wise, will insist upon doing so, and to us, therefore, it seems a pity that Mr. Cross should have gone out of his way to take upon his shoulders, broad as they are, a burden not only too big to be gracefully carried, but which, of necessity, imparts to an otherwise great biography a controversial air as of a man perpetually supporting a thesis *contra mundum.*

When all is said, Lady Mary Wortley Montagu, sprightly dame though she was, and not always on her oath, knew her cousin as he existed in the flesh better than any of us can hope to do, and, being intensely interested in him, has managed to transmit down to us a good piece of his personality, both through herself and through her daughter, Lady Bute, and her granddaughter, Lady Louisa Stuart.

But no sooner have we lodged this complaint, the only one we have to make against Mr. Cross, than fairness compels us to lodge a *caveat* against our own complaint ; for it may be asked of us, What do you mean by this Fielding Tradition ? What is it ? And where are we to look for it ? Not, surely, in the muck-heaps of eighteenth-century journalism—much better left undisturbed and unknown—or in the blind, though intensely amusing jealousy of the author of " Clarissa Harlowe," or in the rancour of Smollett, or even in the vapidities of Murphy ? But if there is anybody still living who, in Henley's picturesque language, sees a " Fielding begrimed with snuff, heady with champagne, and smoking so ferociously that out of the wrappings of his tobacco he could keep himself in paper for the manuscripts of his plays," or even any one who mistakes Thackeray's character-sketch in " The English Humourists " as a serious bit of portrait painting, why then, for such a misguided person, the destructive criticism of Fielding's latest biographer may have its uses, though somewhat marring the symmetry of his picture.

Time mellows Tradition, and on the whole, and as things now stand, Fielding has no more reason than Richardson to quarrel with his tradition, and we feel sure he is content with it. Hence his smile.

For even in his own day, when Arthur Murphy, his first biographer, who had, as Mr. Cross is never tired of telling us, " none of the instincts of the biographer," comes at the close of his " Essay on the Life and Genius of Henry Fielding, Esquire," to sum up his author's career, what do we find him writing ?

In short, our author was unhappy, but not vicious in his nature ; in his understanding lively, yet solid ; rich in invention, yet a lover of real science ; an observer of mankind, yet a scholar of enlarged reading ; a spirited enemy, yet an indefatigable friend ; a satirist of vice and evil, yet a lover of mankind ; a useful citizen, a polished and instructive wit, and a magistrate zealous for the order and welfare of the community he served.

Though this stilted passage may not reveal " the instincts of the biographer," it is none the less sound sense ; and though it falls short of the justice of the case, it conveys in accents of sincerity a friendly judgment upon a great man ; and even the rancorous Smollett, when he lays down the poisoned pen of the hack journalist, and composes his " History," says finely : " The genius of Cervantes was transfused into the novels of Fielding, who painted the characters and ridiculed the follies of the age with equal strength, humour and propriety." This is good criticism, and from a rival novelist generous praise.

To all lovers of the three novels, of the " Miscellanies," and of the " Life of Mr. Jonathan Wild the Great," that masterpiece of irony, particularly pungent in these days ; of that great burlesque, " The Tragedy of Tragedies ; or, the Life and Death of Tom Thumb," and of that unique and moving volume, " Journal of a Voyage to Lisbon," we cordially recommend this " History " of the Father of the English Novel as a noble tribute to a great author.

XIV.

THE LAST DAYS OF QUEEN ELIZABETH.*

(1920.)

THIS is an unusual kind of book, consisting, as it does, of a *précis* (though employing the actual words of the author) of the letters of a most voluminous scribe who lived in the wild, often called the " spacious," days of Queen Elizabeth. The *précis* is accompanied by a careful annotation that explains after a downright, honest, naval fashion most of the incidents, grave or trivial, mentioned in the extracts themselves.

Who, then, was this John Chamberlain whose private correspondence is thus exposed to the general public of 1920 ? In the " Dictionary of National Biography," which always begins its biographies by attempting to describe the subject of each memoir, as, *e.g.*, soldier, sailor, tinker, tailor, or what not, John Chamberlain is described

* " The Life and Times of John Chamberlain." By Edward P. Statham (Retired Commander, R.N.). (Kegan Paul & Co., 1920.)

in one word, " a letter-writer." Was ever before an Englishman thus curtly described ?

Horace Walpole, whose name instantly presents itself when letters are mentioned, is described in the same great compilation as " author, wit, and letter-writer." But Chamberlain composed no book, and though he is often to be found repeating bad jokes, he seems never to have made one, either good or bad, on his own account. He swings, gibbeted, as a letter-writer, and nothing else.

One other description might indeed have been allotted him. He was a Cockney pure and simple, and in the only document, not a letter, that carries his signature—viz., his last will and testament— he directs that his body should be " buried in the parish of St. Olave's in the Old Jewry, where I was born and christened, and where my father, my mother, my brother Robert, and other friends are interred." The date of Chamberlain's birth was January, 1554, and of his burial, March 20th, 1628.

He took but one long journey in his life—to Venice, but of that magic city,

> Where the merchants were the Kings,
> Where St. Mark's is, where the Doges used to wed the sea with
> rings,

he tells us, so far as appears, never a word. We

hear of visits to the Lyttons at Knebworth and to friends at Ascot, but for the most part he was well content to live and die within the sound of Bow Bells.

His father, Richard, was a well-to-do iron-monger and Alderman of the City, and his mother was the daughter of another Alderman. Richard Chamberlain boasted a coat-of-arms, has a fine tomb in St. Olave's Church, and begot thirteen children, of whom the letter-writer was the ninth. All the children were carefully provided for, and John, who was a delicate lad, was specially commended to the "loving and friendly" care of a member of the Grocers' Company!

This is, indeed, a City lineage even more resplendent than that of another Cockney, a good deal Chamberlain's junior, Robert Herrick, who was born in his father's shop in Cheapside and was baptised in 1591 at St. Vedast's, Foster Lane.

Very little is known of John Chamberlain except that he was for a time at Trinity College, Cambridge, and was (probably) a member of Gray's Inn. He never married. He followed no profession; and, indeed, until he began to write letters when over forty, he seems to have done nothing; yet when he did take up his pen his industry was prodigious. Many of his letters—and piles of them are still preserved in the Record Office—have been printed in divers collections, and have long been known to the curious. As a letter-writer he had one great and rare merit, he wrote an excellent and legible hand.

His other merits are hard to discover. Despite his love of gossip, and living as he always did near Paul's Cross, he enjoyed, as a collector of gossip, great advantages, he seems a colourless person. He tells us of

> Pure crude facts
> Secreted from man's life, when hearts beat hard
> And brains, high-blooded, ticked three centuries since ;

of Gunpowder Plots, of Overbury Murders, of Raleigh's execution, of the Essex Divorce Suit, of the Peacham Case, and he does it all with an even pen and exhibits no symptoms of a beating heart or a ticking brain ; and as for religious feeling, there is never a trace, though a new one was in course of manufacture, unless indeed his dread of the Jesuits and his hearty distrust of the old religion can be accounted to him for righteousness.

None the less, this entire absence of " temperature " does not destroy the judicious reader's interest in these letters, for we learn from them how possible it is for the majority of men, then as now, to pass away the time, and lead quiet, and even dull, lives amidst the most astounding tragedies.

The latter days of our great Queen Elizabeth were encased and shrouded in a profound melancholy. Troubles encompassed her on all sides. Even Ireland, that one bright spot in our national existence, was aflame. The Earl of Tyrone held for a moment, and more than for a moment, Dublin at his mercy, having slain two thousand of the Queen's best forces, though London remained, according to Chamberlain, apathetic ; an apathy which he shrewdly attributed not to either courage or wit, but rather " to a careless and insensible dullness." The condition of the Exchequer was as bad as it is to-day. Spain and the Low Countries kept the Foreign Office in a state of continual distraction. The Jesuits were busy with their plots. Scandals of a terrible kind were common topics. And all the time Elizabeth knew her end was approaching. Six days after her death, in March, 1603, Chamberlain writes :

I have not written since I received yours of the 8th, for we here were held in suspense, and know not how or what to write, the passages being stopped, and all conveyance so dangerous and suspitious. I make no question but you have heard of our great loss before this comes to you, and no doubt but you shall hear Her Majesty's sickness and manner of death directly related ; for even here the Papists do tell strange stories as utterly void of truth as of all civil honesty or humanity. I had good means to understand how the world went, and find her disease to be nothing but a confirmed and unremovable melancholie, insomuch that she could not be won nor persuaded neither by the Counsaile, divers phisitians, nor the women about her to taste or touch any phisick, though ten or twelve physitians that were continually about her, did assure her with all manner of asseverations of perfect and entire recovery if she would follow their advice. So that it cannot be said of her as it was of the Emperor Adrian, that *turba medicorum occidit regem*, for they say she died only for lack of phisick : here was some whispering that her braine was somewhat distempered, but there was no such matter, only she held an obstinate silence for the most part, and because she had a persuasion that if she once lay down she should never rise, could not be gotten to bed in a whole week, till three days before her death ; so that after three weeks' languishing she departed the 24th of this present, being our Ladies Eve, between two and three in the morning, as she was born on our Ladies Eve, and as one Lee was Mayor of London, when she came to her Crown, so is there one Lee Mayor now she left it.

The dying Queen, haunted by horror, was not likely to derive any great comfort from the Cockney coincidence about the two Lees !

King James's succession lifted none of the gloom that darkened the bedside of his famous predecessor. Money was tighter than ever, and foreign affairs more confusing. Scandal succeeded scandal. The Overbury Case, with its unspeakable infamies, in which the highest figures both of

Church and State were deeply immersed, might make a Borgia either blush or gnash his teeth with envy, according to his momentary humour.

Here is a line about Sir Walter Raleigh :

I remember that in my last letter I said that Sir Walter Raleigh was not secure, but now he is past peradventure, for on Thursday morning he was beheaded in the old palace of Westminster twixt the Parliament house and the Church . . . the people were much affected at the sight, insomuch that one was heard to say that we had not such another head to cut off.

Although Chamberlain had not a light touch and was no doubt wise not " to let himself go," even had he felt any inclination in those dangerous directions, yet queer incidents, unexpected occurrences, and those odd characters which always lend charm to a personal narrative, keep cropping up. What, for example, can be more unexpected than a cuckoo at St. Paul's ? " Dr. Milwoode, preaching at Powle's Crosse, in the middest of his sermon a cuckowe came flying over the pulpit (a thing I never saw nor heard of before) and very lewdly called and cried out with open mouth."

And as for oddities, who can ever have been odder than Richard Haydock, of Winchester and New College, Oxford, who Chamberlain describes as " the sleeping Preacher so much followed and admired in Oxford " ? Haydock, though a medical man by profession, took to the pulpit, but not being content with the orthodox practice of sending his congregations to sleep, went to sleep himself, and preached eloquent sermons in a state of complete coma. Oxford, ever fond of novelties, went mad over the "sleeping preacher," who, however, when he moved up to the Metropolis, was roughly handled by our learned King, who forced him to make a public recantation of his imposture. This recantation once made, James so far relented as to promise Haydock, if he became a regular divine, preferment in the Church, but this the doctor wisely declined, and spent the rest of his days practising his original profession in Salisbury, where he was never accounted any sleepier than the rest of his Wiltshire neighbours and patients.

To the careful and curious reader this edition of Chamberlain's letters may be safely recommended, though as for the man himself we can only say, with Browning :

The soul doubtless is immortal, when a soul can be discerned.

XV.

THE " QUARTERLY REVIEW "
AND LITERATURE.

(1890.)

THE genuine Quarterly Reviewer, the true breed, is never so happy as when he is mounted on his high horse, trampling over the mob—the now, alas! enfranchised mob.   In his heart of hearts he is still the same creature as he or she who reviewed " Jane Eyre " in the December number, 1849.   He still regrets the levelling spirit of the age, still abhors equality, still believes in bobs and curtseys, and in the divine right of the upper classes to be reverenced by the lower.

He may be found, a mournful and, it must be owned, dilapidated figure, in a recent number of the venerable periodical for which alone he writes. His subject is " Penny Fiction," and his lament— for he is for ever lamenting—is the shocking bad taste in letters of the average Board School boy.

This boy, it appears, has the impudence
to prefer—so the Quarterly Reviewer, on what
authority we know not, asserts—" Spring-heeled
Jack ; or, the Terror of London " to the fascinating Journal of Lady Brassey. This, if true, is
sad ; but there were once reviewers in the land,
of mature years and University training, who
preferred the poetry of the Rev. Mr. Milman and
the Rev. Mr. Atherstone (author of that stirring
work " The Fall of Nineveh ") to the poetry of
John Keats. The admiring reader of " Spring-
heeled Jack " left school for the factory or the
workshop aged thirteen. It would be decent to
show him some little consideration.

This boy also reads—so, at least, we are assured
—" Sweeney Todd, the Demon Barber of Fleet
Street "—a gruesome tale, which the Quarterly
Reviewer denounces as in most atrocious taste,
but which, as stated by him, is not nearly so bad
as a famous Ingoldsby Legend which tells of the
diet of some eels in a pond. But Mr. Barham was
a clergyman of the Establishment. Then there is
" Cheeky Charlie ; or, What a Boy can Do," and
" Turnpike Dick "—two books in which Beaks
and Bobbies, and other constituted authorities
whom all good boys should love are spoken of

contemptuously, and which yet are largely read by State-educated children.

The whole article is tremendously overdone. " Spring-heeled Jack," sad trash as it doubtless is, becomes a count in the indictment against School Boards. This is the result of teaching poor boys to read. Instead of devouring " Murray's Family Library " during the dinner hour or on Sunday mornings, they betake themselves to a kind of fiction which is sold in the neighbourhood of Fleet Street, and is unknown to the publishers of " Don Juan."

Penny fiction is stupid enough ; whether it is stupider than shilling fiction it would be hard to determine. It seems unlikely. But to denounce it, as does this Quarterly Reviewer, as foul and filthy trash, is to speak in King Cambyses' vein. " Spring-heeled Jack " is well within the law. You may be as dull as you please in print, but you must not be either obscene or blasphemous. " Spring-heeled Jack " observes this law better than many.

People who lead hard, dull lives are not content with the " Harvest of a Quiet Eye," or the " Diary of an Invalid." They love excitement, and, if they are taught to read at all, will read exciting books.   Then the question arises, What is an exciting book ? Upon this a Board School boy is entitled to be as tenacious of his opinion as Quarterly Reviewers are of theirs.

Nobody nowadays reads " The Mirror of Knighthood," which is the English translation, in nine volumes, of the Spanish romance, once in Don Quixote's library, " Espeio de Principes y Cavalleros."   It would be rather difficult to read it, even were one so minded, for Mr. Bullen, in his Preface to " Lyrics from Elizabethan Romances," tells us that only one perfect copy is known to exist, and that is in the Bodleian, where reading is discouraged.   But in Elizabeth's days, adds Mr. Bullen, using a phrase I venture to deprecate, for it smacks of " the trade,"

the book was highly esteemed, particularly by romantic 'prentices and waiting-maids. Sir Thomas Overbury, in his character of " A Chambermaid," tells us, " She reads Greene's works over and over, but is so carried away with ' The Mirror of Knighthood ' she is many times resolved to run out of herself and become a lady-errant."

According to the Quarterly Reviewer, the perusal of " Spring-heeled Jack " and " Turnpike Dick " has just the same effect upon our Board School boys.   They long to take to the road.

The " Mirror of Knighthood " appeared in parts,

like " Pickwick " and " Vanity Fair," and was no
doubt considered at the time, and probably with
justice, to be a vain and amatorious work and one
well calculated to demoralise the masses, who,
however, found in it a narcotic for their pain.
The Curate of La Mancha, it will be remembered,
was disposed to save it from the flames because it
had some part in the inventions of Boiardo and
Ariosto. Mr. Ormsby tells us that next to the
history of Charlemagne and the Twelve Peers, it
was the most popular of the Carlovingian series of
romances. It lived to turn the heads of English
chambermaids in the time of Elizabeth, and now
of the English version there is but one perfect
copy known to exist, and that is in the Bodleian.
What, one may well ask, is Fame ?

As long as the world remains what hitherto it
has always been, people will read, as Sir Thomas
Overbury's chambermaid read the " Mirror of
Knighthood," not to improve their minds, but in
order " to run out of themselves." Those books
will ever be the world's favourites which make
their readers run fastest.

There is an immense deal of clap-trap talked,
and more written, about books and reading—the
Ministry of Books, the Consolations of Literature,

and I know not what other fine phrases. Some of
the finest may be often encountered pilloried in
the catalogues of the second-hand booksellers,
who, being lawfully desirous of turning over their
stock quickly, are fond of appending to a terse
description of the particular volumes for sale some
luscious quotation describing the immense consolation the work in question has been to some
person or another. Thus, the voice of that highly
scandalous prelate, Bishop Watson, is often to be
heard through the land asserting, under the head
of Locke, " Let them (the works of John, in ten
volumes, octavo) be ever on your table, and when
you have an hour to spend from business or
pleasure, spend it with them." That is not the
way the Bishop of Llandaff spent his very ample
leisure. " The Anatomy of Melancholy " is
monthly advertised in a score of catalogues as the
only book that ever got Dr. Johnson out of bed
two hours sooner than he wished to rise. What
evidence is there worth having that Dr. Johnson
ever in his life got out of bed in order to read
old Burton's " Anatomy " ? It is true that he
is reported to have told the Rev. Dr. Maxwell,
" some time assistant preacher at the Temple," that
such was the case ; and had the statement been

that the book had prevented him going to bed for two hours after he had better have been there, I should have had no difficulty in believing it. But as it stands it savours of the unreality which infests this subject.

As for the consolation, who was ever consoled in real trouble by the small beer of literature or science ? It is Dr. Newman asks the question, not I.

Literature should be taken seriously, but not too seriously. " Robinson Crusoe " may have sent some boys to sea, Franklin's " Poor Richard " may have made some youths thrifty, but this is not the usual process of manufacture. Many a gallant soldier has a vile taste in letters. General Wolfes are rare. The Duke of Wellington seems to have read next to nothing. Gordon was fond of Bogatsky's " Golden Treasury." Some of our greatest judges have been very partial to the trashiest kind of novel. The vulgar and odious language of the street often defiles and defames, but cannot destroy, kind thoughts and generous actions. Bookishness is an intellectual monkery. It is the criticism of the cloister. In the beginning it has a charm, this devotedness to books and what people have said, but after a time it becomes

wearisome and an offence, and you long to meet
some child of Nature who has never read anything
and cannot torture you with endless quotations,
or thrust borrowed opinions down your throat.   In
such moments the frank candour of a schoolboy,
his " beastlys " and " jollys," are more refreshing
than the most elaborate appreciations.

Still, the great thing is to keep pegging away
with cheap masterpieces.   The good books will
beat the bad ones ;   they always have, and,
despite our dolorous Quarterly Reviewer, they
always will.   The boy does not breathe who will
not prefer " The Three Musketeers " to " Spring-
heeled Jack," although he may prefer " Spring-
heeled Jack " to Dean Burgon's " Twelve Good
Men " ; but cheap books, however good, will not
give a town-born and a town-bred population the
thews and sinews of a conquering race, neither
will they make virtue easy or rob death of a single
terror.

XVI.

THE "EDINBURGH REVIEW" AND RELIGION.

(1890.)

AMIDST the clash of contending dogmas and the hot rivalry of sects, the fervent Sacramentarianism of one bishop, and the fierce Evangelicalism of another, it is at least amusing to be reminded of the continued existence in our midst of a body of men whose zeal for their religion, if measured by the strength of their antipathies, is great; and who are able even in these bad, unbelieving days to solace their souls and satisfy every religious aspiration they possess by daily non-attendance at the services of their beloved Church. The institution which attracts these Christian heroes, and which enjoys the benefit of their expletives, is, we need hardly add, the Church of England, as by law established within this realm. One of these pious souls has been moved, in the columns of a recent number of the *Edinburgh Review*, to attempt a comparison between the lives of Dr. Newman, of the Oratory, Birmingham, and Dr. Lightfoot, of the See of Durham, both divines lately deceased, in which the Roman gentleman gets very much the worst of it. The writer of the article in question, if he has any real acquaintance with the works of either Newman or Lightfoot, does himself injustice, for his treatment of this part of his subject is miserably meagre ; but the charm and interest of the article—and it is both charming and interesting—consists in the naïve and sincere revelation which it makes of the religious plight of its excellent and patriotic, though ill-instructed, author, who may be taken as a fair specimen of his class.

To start with, this Edinburgh Reviewer cannot away with dogma. It worries him and makes him uncomfortable after the same fashion as Mr. Robert Lowe was made uncomfortable by the sermons of Dr. Pusey. He feels somewhere in the neighbourhood of his midriff that he is a Church-of-England man ; not so much because he believes that our Lord was born of a virgin, as the Creeds confidently recite, as because of his honest hatred of Papists and Dissenters and the Religion of Humanity. Hence his dislike of dogma and consequent abomination of Newman, who, poor, unhappy boy, started life with the false notion that it was a matter of terrible importance to believe aright—whereas, says this reviewer, it is really a matter of quite secondary importance as compared with sticking by the dear old Church of England. This is how he puts it :

> The falsehood with which Dr. Newman started in life, which he never got rid of, and which vitiated his whole subsequent career, was the idolatry of dogma. . . . But people who really read their New Testament have long ago come to the serenest faith that the world is managed by God on principles quite different from these.

Is this serene faith of our reviewer the doctrine of the Church of England ? It certainly seems addressed to a nation of shopkeepers. Small profits and quick returns as opposed to high prices and long credit. But it is a touching and genuinely sincere tribute to Divine Management. The reviewer continues in the same strain and grows bolder as he proceeds, until at last he essays to define Christianity, a task which he finds as easy as it is (in his opinion) to be a Christian. Says he :

> To believe in Christ and to be sure that while He abhors and will condemn proselyte-hunting and the absorption of the person into an impersonal system, He smiles on all fair inquiry and pardons every honest doubt—is Christianity.

What a picture, to be sure ! Christ hung upon
the tree in order to smile on " fair inquiry " and
pardon " honest doubt." He abhors proselyte-
hunting, and is anxious to preserve individual
peculiarities ; and this, if you please, is Christianity in the columns of the *Edinburgh Review*.
What, we wonder, would Dr. Lightfoot have had
to say of such a definition of Christianity as this ?
It would have made his gorge rise, and have been
as repulsive to him as to Dr. Newman. Is there a
bishop or divine of the Church of England who
would not repudiate and condemn such a vulgar
travesty of religion ?

But Church-of-Englandism is far too robust, too
secular-minded, to care a rap about the opinion of
bishops and divines, who are but necessary evils,
only to be defended when attacked by low-minded
Radicals and vulgar Dissenters. It is the external
church, the bricks and mortar, the ivy-mantled
tower, nestling in the valley hard by the " Blue
Boar," the chiming of the bells on a Sunday morning as they fall on the ears of men walking in an
opposite direction, that appeal to these stalwart
sons of the Establishment. The Church they love
is neither the Church of Bishop King nor of Bishop
Ryle ; it is no holy vessel containing the precious

deposit of dogma which gleams through the discourses of Mr. Gore ; it is none of these things, but, in the glowing language of its *Edinburgh* eulogist, it is

A Church which is so conscious of her veracity and her faith towards God that she fears not the world at all ; a Church whose Chief Pastor goes in and out of Lambeth Palace at all hours of the day and night without guards and without temporary power ; a Church which, like most of the Protestant Communions, can afford to ride freely to the anchor of the ancient creeds, because she is afloat and not aground, and can afford to repent of her past sins and present errors, since she makes no preposterous claim to be infallible.

In this passage our enthusiast too obviously confuses the boundaries which separate the sublime from the ridiculous. The spectacle he invites us to behold of Dr. Benson letting himself into Lambeth Palace at two in the morning, " without guards," lacks grandeur, and provokes the remark that, as the Archbishop, like the apostle Peter, is a married man, even his nocturnal prowlings cannot fairly be described as entirely unguarded. Dr. Newman once forgot himself so far as to inquire anxiously whether Dr. Arnold was a Christian. It is happily not necessary to direct the same inquiry as to this Edinburgh Reviewer, for his strong point is not his Christianity, but his Church-of-Englandism. Like the Church of his

mature affections, he rides so freely to the anchor
of his ancient creeds that we are at times forced to
believe that he has slipped it altogether. Nor does
his frank avowal that the next century will laugh
at " old-world theology " allay our anxiety on this
score. But it is idle to argue such points with men
like this reviewer, who are for the Church of
England because it is not the Church of Rome—
who will only consume home-made articles—who
will wear neither helmet nor shield nor any of the
armour of God unless it is stamped with the broad
arrow—who, in short, are Church of England men
first and anything they please afterwards. To men
of this mould, to cease to belong to the Church of
England is to be a renegade from the national
flag—to go over to the enemy.   Church-of-
Englandism is the religion of England, and it is
the duty of every Englishman to belong to the
English religion. What that religion is doesn't
matter, and is perhaps uncertain. But, whatever
it is, it is a moderate, decent religion which leaves
you alone, or which you can leave alone if so
minded. We feel certain this Edinburgh Reviewer
has not been inside a church for a twelve-month.

XVII.

THE AGE OF VICTORIA—THE AGE OF LAW REFORM.

(1897.)

WE are great babies! It is hardly to be supposed that any one will be at the pains to dispute a proposition which does not involve either personal unsightliness or any remarkable degree of moral obliquity. Her most Gracious Majesty (whom God preserve) has occupied the throne of these realms for a longer time than any of her predecessors. She is, therefore, a record-breaker, and up go the hats of a nation of sportsmen, as gamblers are now called. Let us join the festival and play the fool with Time, who eventually will play a trick upon us that will, if it does not stop our moralisings altogether, at least give them a new direction. *To moralise*—this is the task of the newspapers at periods like the present, and right gallantly are their chartered scribes discharging it. It is scribble, scribble, scribble all day long, and

all night too.   Estimates and appreciations of the
Victorian Age spring daily into existence.   It is
being treated on all sides from every point of
view.   Its poets, its dramatists, its historians, its
medical men, its actors, its warriors, its divines,
its statesmen, the course of its trade, wholesale and
retail, its paupers, its millionaires, its education,
its crime.   Like Mrs. Siddons' nose, there is no end
to it.

And now for my little contribution.   I have no
desire to disparage other scribes and other ideas.
But, I may observe, I stand on safe ground.   I
suppose everybody—unless he is a hero, poet, or
a publisher—will admit that all our greatest poets,
dramatists, actors, warriors, historians, philosophers, orators, divines, took the unmannerly pre-
caution to live and die outside the limits of the
Victorian Age.   No need for a Royal Commission
to bring out the facts; they are at hand.   The
Victorian Age boasts but one name of universal
fame—Charles Darwin.   It may be that two or
three other names in the same realm of science
might be mentioned in a society of experts with a
good chance not only of recognition, but of
acknowledgment, of their great claims ; but it does
not do to be technical on really popular occasions.

Shove yourself forward in fancy another hundred years. Bear in mind what must be the huge output of its energies; think of the libraries it will compose, the pictures it will paint; consider its new buildings, its new inventions, its hurrying industries and crowded paths; reflect how soon phrases become first familiar, then stale, and finally repulsive, and how little leisure men have for research, and how averse they grow to devote time to the comprehension of abandoned positions and antiquated tastes, and then put yourself this question : What production of the Victorian Age is so finished, so beautiful, and so strong as to be able successfully to meet and beat down the huge and swamping spring-tide of the days that are to come ?

If you want to back the winner for the Victorian Stakes you must put your money, not on the wrong horse, but on the right one, and his name is Law Reform.

Do not, we beseech you, gentle and loyal reader, sniff contemptuously at my steed, or hastily assert that you would sooner put your money on a spavined snail than on my rawboned beast,

Thrust out past service from the Devil's stud.

Keep your temper and look at it first. 'Tis a

useful if not a showy animal. Anyhow, it is my choice, and I ask your patience for a few minutes whilst I enumerate its points.

In 1837 Her Majesty ascended the throne. The Court of Chancery then existed. If you want to know what the Court of Chancery was like, read " Bleak House," by Charles Dickens. Doctors Commons then existed. If you want to know what Doctors Commons was like, read " David Copperfield," by Charles Dickens. In the fourteen months from October, 1838, to December, 1839, 3,905 persons were arrested for debt in London, of whom 361 were permanently detained in a debtors' gaol. If you want to know what a debtors' gaol was like, read " Little Dorrit," by Charles Dickens. And if anybody tells you Charles Dickens exaggerates, tell him, with my compliments, he is, in parliamentary language, an ignoramus, and in plain English, a fool.* The crowning achievement of the Victorian Age was the establishment of one high court administering the same law to the suitor who either sought justice or resisted iniquity. The spectacle of two independent,

* If any one doubts Dickens let him read " A History of the Court of Chancery," 1828, by the celebrated " Jo Parkes," the friend of Hazlitt and an experienced solicitor and excellent writer. It is a learned work.

mutually jealous and ever hostile judicatures, one giving legal and the other equitable relief—both systems being highly technical and terribly expensive—at last ceased to insult the common-sense of the nation. Now, go where he will, or let him be taken where he may, the litigant finds one law. It was a great day in the history of England, December 4th, 1882, when the Queen opened the Royal Courts of Justice.

Procedure, too, merciful heavens, how it has been knocked about ! It is enough to make the dry bones of grand old Jeremy Bentham come out of their cupboard in Gower Street and join the procession this month. The Judicature Acts and the new practice have saved millions of money and destroyed a system of legalised injustice which almost seemed as if it meant to defy mankind. " It may be asserted," said the late Lord Bowen, a lawyer who loved the light, " without fear of contradiction, that it is not possible in the year 1887 for an honest litigant in Her Majesty's supreme Court to be defeated by any mere technicality, any slip, any mistake made in the litigation." Shade of Baron Parke, what do you say to that ? Improvements are still possible, some are even urgent, but the dry rubbish has been shot. The

Judicature Acts of Queen Victoria are great epoch-marking triumphant measures. What shall we say about county courts? Let the poor man answer. They need improvement, but every day they are improving, and who can deny that they place the supreme force of the State at the disposal of the humblest of Her Majesty's subjects? When the Queen traverses the Borough she may proudly rest assured, as she gazes on the crowd of upturned faces, that there can hardly be one of them that has not been " county-courted." It is laws like this that really cut deep into the life of a nation. Your Newcastle Programmes are but the fireworks of politics. Judicature Acts and County Court Acts shape our destinies and mould our minds.

Another great achievement must be briefly mentioned : the Law of Evidence.

Again, I beseech you, do not sniff. The Law of Evidence lies at the bottom of the well. How to get at the Truth ? It is really more important than Frank Frenzy's last ode or little Mr. Twitter's triolet. Our old pre-Victorian law rejected evidence wholesale. No interested person could be called as a witness. As has been wittily said, " If a farmer in his gig ran over a foot-passenger in the road, the two persons whom the law single out to prohibit from becoming witnesses were the farmer and the foot-passenger." Good Queen Victoria altered all this ; and now, with hardly any exception, the people who know most about the facts in issue can be called to tell the court what they do know about them. No doubt there is more perjury than there used to be. Interested parties will tell lies, but there are ways of testing liars.

Two other gigantic institutions cutting very deep indeed into our national life sprang into existence during the Victorian Age : limited liability companies and the Divorce Court ! " Where is your Wully Shakespeare now ? " one may almost exclaim. Carlyle alone of the men of this century, Swift alone of the far greater eighteenth-century team, could do justice to this strange pair, fraught with so many things, laden with so many consequences. Neither the Divorce Court nor companies limited by shares are fit subjects for indiscriminate eulogy. I confess to thinking the Divorce Court the most odious place in Great Britain. Mr. Wordsworth has assured us that

> One impulse from a vernal wood
> Will teach us more of man,
> Of moral evil and of good,
> Than all the sages can.

I have sometimes laid down Mr. Buckley's immortal treatise of the Companies' Acts and fled
into a wood, and there listened to the cooing of the
doves and caught sight of the squirrels running to
their sylvan homes; but I have sorrowfully to
confess that as a student of moral evil I have
learnt more from (let me say) the twenty-fifth
section of the Companies' Act, 1867, than from all
the woods and forests I have ever visited at home
and abroad.

But I must leave for others the moralising, and
press on.

The legal position of women—what do you say
to that? It has been revolutionised in the reign
of a woman. The Married Woman's Property
Act, 1882, is a measure the social importance of
which it is impossible to exaggerate.

Roughly speaking, before that Act a married
woman could have no property, save by the inter-
vention of trustees or by an equitable doctrine.
Now marriage makes no difference. Before the
Act, John and Jane stood before the altar; Jane
had £1,000 to her credit at the London and
County Bank, a leasehold house in the neighbourhood of the Addison Road, furniture, books,
prints, plate, etc., and £100 in her pocket. The

wedding was without settlements and without cards. Service fully choral. Result—that when John and Jane left the church, Jane's £1,000, Jane's leasehold house, Jane's furniture, books, prints, plate, etc., and Jane's pretty little purse in her absurdly situated pocket, all had become John's. After the Act, what was Jane's remains Jane's. Here is a difference, indeed ; not only in fact, but in feeling. The same thing with regard to the after-acquired property of a wife. Before the Act, with few exceptions, it became the husband's ; his receipt alone was a full discharge. After the Act, the wife's receipt alone is a full discharge. So, too, with the earnings of a married woman ; they are Jane's, not John's. Poor Mr. Mantalini ! The amount of barbarous cruelty and downright highway robbery practised by the Mantalinis of the past upon industrious wives is incalculable. The Chancery Bar used to know a good deal about it in the old days, and to lawyers these reforms are largely due. The electorate (poor things !) seldom hear of anything really important.

Another cognate subject must be noticed : the rights of mothers to their children. Queen Victoria was the first sovereign to recognise the existence of these rights. By the common law, children, if born in wedlock, are the property of the father. If born out of wedlock, a child has no father, and therefore, lest it should become derelict, belongs to the mother. The excellent Blackstone observes, " Mothers, *as such*, are entitled to no power, only reverence and respect." There was a pretty weapon for husbands. " Unless you give me my way, I will take away my children, who happen also, according to the course of Nature, though not of the courts, to be yours as well."

I have not room to recount the anguish of mothers recorded in our grim law books, or I could make you

Weep afresh a long since cancelled woe.

Not, indeed, that it was cancelled so very long ago, but it does not do to take liberties with a line of Shakespeare's. The necessary reforms began in 1839, and were completed in 1891. During the same period mothers were enabled to appoint guardians to their infant children.

The women of England may justly regard the Victorian Age as the time of their *Magna Charta*.

Have I not made good my nomination ? In matters of greater technicality, but still of vast importance and far-reaching effects, the Age has

been remarkable. As a bit of workmanlike legis-
lation, the Lands Clauses Consolidation Act of
1845, and the Railway Acts of the same period,
stand out in bold relief. By them and under their
businesslike provisions this Merry England of ours
has become a huge gridiron of railways. The very
first year of the Queen's reign saw placed upon the
Statute Book the Wills Act, which still governs
our testamentary dispositions, whilst in recent
days we have seen a series of codifying statutes
relating to such subjects as bills of exchange, sale
of goods, partnership, merchant shipping become
law, to the great advantage of the community, and
affording a happy augury of a good time coming
when both our civil and our criminal law shall be
found in a code.

The Age of Victoria has been, I repeat it, an
Age of Law Reform. Looking back upon it, one
cannot discern much method or system. Things
have to take their chance in a free country. In
our rough island story there has been no Justinian.
But in the retrospect, gazing back upon the savage
country through which we have passed, we have
no difficulty in marking the progress we have
made, and when we look forward need we doubt
that we shall, in the future, go quicker and

straighter to the goal of all honest endeavour ? What that goal is all are agreed—the honest, cheap, and speedy administration of a just and certain body of law.

In the history of our journey to this goal, the reign of Queen Victoria must always occupy the foremost place. From this position she can never be dispossessed.

XVIII.

OLD NOLLEKENS.

(1920.)

Well, sir, I think my friend Joe Nollekens can chop out a head with any of them.

DR. JOHNSON.

THE two volumes of the Life of Joseph Nollekens by John Thomas Smith, keeper of the prints and drawings in the British Museum from 1816 to 1833, first published by Colburn (a publisher to whom we owe much) in 1828, have ever since that date been greatly prized by the "miscellaneous writer" as storehouses of quotable matter ever ready to his hand. Another book by the same hand, bearing the fascinating title "A Book for a Rainy Day," has enjoyed the same recognition. A couple of anecdotes out of "Rainy Day" Smith's publications, about some artist dead and gone, or some bit of "Old London" long since ruthlessly destroyed, were quite enough in days gone by to establish a "Fleet Street" reputation for considerable erudition and an unusually wide

range of reading. May those perish who reprint
our sources of information ! But we ought not
to be selfish in such matters, and, as we find ourselves growing old and rusty in the business, it is
easy to regard with pleasure the handsome and
admirable edition of Smith's Life of Nollekens
which Mr. Wilfred Whitten has lately seen through
the Press.* Well, indeed, does Mr. Whitten refer
to " Rainy Day " Smith as " this useful and amusing man, whose anecdotes have irrigated so many
books." *Irrigated !* 'Tis the very word ! Smith's
anecdotes have watered many hundreds of acres
of dry and dusty print. They crop up, again and
again, in book after book, and usually without
acknowledgment, as if springing spontaneously
from the author's memory, and, like Cowper's rills,

> With a livelier green
> Betray the secret of their silent course.

The battered and dingy tribe of miscellaneous
writers had indeed at one time good cause to be
thankful for " Rainy Day " Smith.

But now, as with that other wandering tribe,
the gypsies, the times are day by day growing
harder than ever with the miscellaneous writer :

> They must live, still, and yet, God knows,
> Crowded and keen the country grows.

* Nollekens and his Times by John Thomas Smith.
Edited by Wilfred Whitten. 2 vols. 1920. (John Lane.)

What with new and annotated editions of old books, long out of print, and of great compilations like the " Dictionary of National Biography," the poor miscellaneous writer who could once earn a meagre living by patching together an article, half biography, half criticism, finds it harder than ever to gain a market for his stale wares, and curses these fine reprints and undertakings as savouring of capitalism and combines.

It was a little unkind of Mr. Gosse, who well knows how hard it is for a miscellaneous writer to live in these days, to be the first editor of Smith's Nollekens in 1895, and thus to expose to the public eye the contents of a larder which for more than half a century had been, to a large extent, reserved for the use of one particular industry. And now Mr. Whitten, equally well informed, comes along, twenty years after Mr. Gosse, with another attractive reproduction ! Charles Lamb felt unhappy when he first saw a modern edition of Burton's " Anatomy of Melancholy " in the booksellers' shops, and we can imagine similar feelings being excited in some apprehensive breasts at the sight of " Old Nollekens " in full dress in Hatchard's.

But there is really no need for the miscellaneous

writer to hang himself. *Magna est ignorantia et prævalebit.* Just as there is always somebody in any audience who has never heard or read anything, and may, therefore, be relied upon to lead the laughter at the stalest joke, so, after a short while, say, a twelve-month hence, there will be small risk in " potting out " old stories from Smith's books, though for a season the miscellaneous writer should, following the pious example of Burns' cottar, " wale his portion with judicious care."

To review Smith's Life of Nollekens is as impossible as it ought to have been for Smith to write it. The book takes high rank among the spiteful biographies, and it is to pass a harsh verdict upon that odd compound, human nature, to have to admit that spitefulness is a better quality in a biographer, from the biographee's point of view, than an amiable, uncritical effusiveness.

Smith was a fortune-hunter after the Roman fashion, made familiar in the comedies of Plautus, and probably from the first hour, when in 1779, as a boy of thirteen, he entered Nollekens' studio as a model for legs and arms, he had his eye upon his master's ducats ; and this interest in the old miser's accumulations never flagged during all the years of his servitude. It is pleasing to be able to relate that " Rainy Day " Smith never got a penny out of the £200,000 Nollekens and his excellent wife (on whom Dr. Johnson is said to have cast the eye of partiality) had scraped together. There was a will and many codicils, but nothing for Smith. Hence the venom of the biographer.

Smith's task of bespattering his old employer was an easy one, for Nollekens had all the notes of the old-fashioned miser, being a coarse-grained fellow, of Dutch extraction, dirty in language and filthy in his personal habits ; whilst his wife, the daughter of Fielding's successor as a London police magistrate, though at one time fair to look upon, was as miserly as her husband.

The pair of them carried economy to the pitch of sublimity, and their malicious biographer does not spare us a single damaging detail. Smith's method strangely reminds me of another spiteful biography, that of Cardinal Manning by Mr. Purcell. One biographer worked in marble, the other in clay, but the method was the same.

Yet, when all that spitefulness can do had been done, the dirty old miser has probably fared better at the hands of this malignant biographer than would have been the case had his Life been written by the usual conventional hand trying his best to conceal all the vitality of the man. The same is true of Manning's biography.

Smith was bound to record some kind, and even generous, actions of the old sculptor that reveal the fact that amidst the squalor and dirt of his miserly existence there was a feeling heart ; and these significant actions, recorded by a grudging witness, " shine like a good deed in a naughty world." A strange and delightful feature about Smith is his passion for the topography of London. His bump of locality triumphs even over his bump of avarice, and he is for ever leaving his old master, stealing his nutmegs at the dinners of the Royal Academy, or wrangling with his cobbler over the nails in a pair of shoes, in order to wander through the streets of old London, a habit he probably learnt from Nollekens, who, in his turn, had been taught it by his mother.

Another time Mr. Nollekens stopped at the corner of Rathbone Place and observed that, when he was a little boy, his mother often took him to the top of that street, to walk by the side of a long pond near a windmill, and that a halfpenny was paid by every person at a hatch (a nursery ground) belonging to the miller, for the privilege of walking in his grounds. He also told me that his mother took him through another halfpenny hatch in the fields between Oxford Road and Grosvenor Square, the north side of which was then building. When we got to the brewhouse between Rathbone Place and the end of Tottenham Court Road, he said he recollected thirteen large and fine walnut trees standing on the north side of the highway (Vol. I., p. 34).

Another quotation :

Mr. Nollekens, on his way to the Roman Catholic Chapel in Duke Street, Lincoln's Inn Fields, where he was christened, stopped to show me the dilapidations of the Duke of Monmouth's house in Soho Square. It was on the south side of the houses which now stand in Bateman's Buildings. Though the workmen were employed in pulling it down, we ventured to go in. The gate entrance was of massive ironwork, supported by stone piers, surmounted by the crest of the owner of the house, and within the gates there was a spacious courtyard. The hall was ascended by steps. There were eight rooms on the ground floor . . . the staircase was of oak. As we ascended I remember Mr. Nollekens noticing the busts of Seneca, Caracalla, Trajan, Adrian, and several others upon brackets. The principal room on the first floor, which had not been disturbed by the workmen, was lined with blue satin, superbly decorated with pheasants and other birds in gold. The chimney-piece was richly ornamented with fruit and foliage similar to the carvings which surround the altar of St. James's Church, Piccadilly, so beautifully executed by Grinling Gibbons, etc., etc. (Vol. I., pp. 27–28).

Walking through London with old Nollekens and the young viper Smith is, indeed, " to moan the expense of many a vanished sight."

Smith can hardly ever mention a man without telling you precisely where he lived. Thus :

Mr. Seward, of anecdote memory, who lodged at the Golden Ball, No. 5, Little Maddox Street, where the sign is still perched was, etc. (Vol. I., p. 141).

Lord Eldon often speaks of the fine fruit in Gower Street which his Lordship enjoyed when he lived in the house now No. 42, and has, indeed, spoken in open Court of the sad effect the London smoke had upon his garden in Gower Street. So late in the year 1800, William Bentham, of No. 6, Upper Gower Street (a gentleman whose well-chosen collection of English Topography is unqestionably the most select and perfect of any formed within my memory), had nearly twenty-five dozen of the finest and most delicious *nectarines,* all fit for the table, gathered from three completely exposed trees.

This last quotation is enough to make the mouths of the fine ladies who have now taken to live in Gower Street to overflow. In such passages we see Smith at his best, and it is only fair to say that they abound.

Saving the exceptions I felt bound to make from the very first, in the interests of a tribe of writers for whom I have a not unnatural affection, for, as Garrick says in one of his inimitable prologues,

A fellow feeling makes one wondrous kind,

I can confidently recommend those who have a liking for biography and topography to make themselves acquainted with Mr. John Thomas Smith, both in his " Nollekens " and his " Rainy Day."

In leaving Mr. Smith I must do so with an anecdote, probably my last theft from his once well-frequented pages. Amongst other pleasing traits in Nollekens' character was his extravagant pleasure in street cries, and the pains he took to acquire both the words and the notes of itinerant vendors. Nollekens shared his taste both with Ned Shuter and Jack Bannister, two famous comedians, whose names (thanks to Charles Lamb) are still familiar to our ears, and it is of Ned Shuter that Bannister told the following story, which Smith repeats :

" Ned was so fond of London cries that he would frequently follow people for hours together to get their cries correctly. I recollect a story he used to tell of his following a man who had a peculiar cry, up one street and down another, nearly a whole day, to get his cry, but the man never cried ; at last, being quite out of temper, he went up to the fellow and said, ' You don't cry—why the devil don't you cry ? ' The man answered in a piteous tone, ' Cry ! Lord bless your heart, sir, I can't cry—my wife's dead ; she died this morning.' "

XIX.

CLERK SCOTT'S DECISIONS.

(1919.)

But instead of writing nonsense, you will expect, no doubt, that I should give you a little news from " Auld Reekie." I presume you will be little edified or entertained by an extract from my new work, which is to be entitled " Clerk Scott's Decisions," and is to come out on cream-coloured, wire-woven paper, printed by Ballantyne, with a vignette to each number, the first to represent Hermand, *rampant*, and Polkemmet, *couchant*, and Bannatyne, *dormant*. (Letter to Adam Ferguson. See " Familiar Letters of Sir Walter Scott," Vol. I., p. 63. Hermand, etc., were three judges of the Court of Session.)

JUSTICE is proverbially slow-footed, and, like the author of " Waverley," hobbles in her gait, but eventually she arrives, and now, in 1919, after waiting patiently for ninety years, justice has been done to Sir Walter Scott in his professional capacity, for in this soberly bound volume, intituled as below,* will be found the reports of all the judgments of that eminent man, delivered by him during the thirty-three years of his tenure

* " Scott's Decisions in the Sheriff Court of Selkirk." By John Chisholm, K.C. (Edinburgh : W. Green & Son, Law Publishers.)

of the judicial office of sheriff of the county of Selkirk.

John Scott, Lord Eldon, has long had his recording angel, and "Vesey's Reports" are as well known in Lincoln's Inn as is Hansard in the Palace of Westminster. The decisions of William Scott, Lord Stowell, are they not written in the pages of "Haggard"? And now, at last, a third and a greater Scott has found his *Vates* in Mr. John Chisholm, and the grave records of a long judicial career are ushered forth in the judge's own romantic town by a firm (mark this) of law publishers.

The sudden appearance of this fascinating book may perhaps awaken the echoes, not indeed of Fontarabia, but of a half-forgotten newspaper controversy, which would long ere this have been entirely forgotten had not that "mad wag," Sir Henry Newbolt, hitched it into rhyme, over the difference between the professional writer and the amateur.

What was Sir Walter's profession? Was it that of a man of letters, who chanced to be called to the bar, or of a man of law, who wrote the Waverley Novels?

It is easy to dispose of this question once for all

and by the best of all processes—dates. Scott was
called to the Scottish Bar in June, 1792, after
producing and publishing a thesis in Latin concerning the disposal of the dead bodies of criminals,
cannily dedicated by the budding lawyer to the
then Lord Justice Clerk, that very Macqueen of
Braxfield, specimens of whose unholy merriment
still linger in northern memories, making a few
laugh and more (I trust) weep. After practising
his profession for seven and a half years, Scott, in
December, 1799, obtained his sheriffdom, and
retained it until his death in 1832.

In addition to this much-coveted post, Scott in
1806—eight years before " Waverley "—became a
clerk in the Court of Session, an office entailing
almost daily attendance during the sittings of the
court, with an annual salary attached to it of
£1,300. This position, akin to that of registrar in
an English court, was filled by Scott until 1830,
and during this long period he was a familiar figure
in the legal world of Edinburgh, and not infrequently had to listen to the judges, sitting above
him, eking out their erudition and enlivening the
tedium of their usual discourse by legal quotations
drawn from the pages of " The Antiquary," " Red-
gauntlet," and " The Heart of Midlothian." If

Sir Walter was not a professional lawyer, who was or is one ?

" The Lay of the Last Minstrel " was not published until 1805, by which date its author had, in the pleasing, if jargonic language of his profession, " assoilzied " scores of " defenders," and sent as many " pursuers " empty away.

The professional lawyer, like Scott, is concerned, either as advocate or judge, with the disputes and malfeasances of other men, and he is usually content to leave the written records of his well-paid labours to the reporters either of the Court or of the Press. When not professionally employed, lawyers and judges amuse themselves after divers fashions.

Many great lawyers have written books on subjects outside the sphere of their profession without exposing themselves to the calumny of having been amateurs. No one will be bold enough to assert that " broad-browed " Verulam was an amateur lawyer ; and yet of those who have read his " Essays " and his " Novum Organum," and the two books " On the Advancement of Learning," how many have studied Bacon's famous reading on the " Statute of Uses " or done full justice to his great argument on the status of men

born in England or Scotland after the accession of
the Scottish king to the English throne ?   In the
case of another versatile Lord Chancellor, Henry
Brougham, though there may be those still living
ready to deny his claim to be considered a great
master of the law, who will dispute that Brougham
was a professional lawyer from the end of his very
sensitive nose to the tips of his predatory fingers ?
And yet Brougham wrote and published a novel
in three volumes, with a title at least as romantic
as any of Sir Walter's.

The position of a Scotch sheriff within his juris-
diction is, and always has been, a proud one, and
to belittle it is to write yourself down, if not an
ass, at least as an ignorant and conceited Southron.
There is a great tradition behind the sheriffdom.
Lord Advocates are not easily moved to emotion,
but I remember seeing one, and a very distinguished one, greatly perturbed when parliamentary pressure was being put upon him to appoint
a good friend of his own to a vacant sheriffdom,
I think, of Perthshire.   He was willing to make
the appointment, and eventually did so—but not
until after the funeral of the late occupant.   This
was all very well, but the Government was totter-
ing to its fall, and even two days' delay might have

lost the patronage. Yet the Lord Advocate held out, observing, in almost broken tones, that it never should be said that during his tenure there were two Sheriffs of Perth above ground at the same time. This proves the greatness of the tradition.

The procedure of the Sheriff Court was by written pleadings, often very racy pleadings, and these pleadings and the proof of the evidence were, in most cases, forwarded to Scott in Edinburgh, where, after reading the papers, he made up his mind and gave his decision in writing, with a succinctness and lucidity not always noticeable in the Waverley Novels. He never gave his reasons.

If either suitor was dissatisfied, he might appeal to the Court of Session or demand a rehearing.

" In all," says Mr. Chisholm, " Sir Walter Scott gave judgment in 114 legal processes, civil and criminal."

I confidently recommend this volume of Reports to all lovers of Scott, and particularly to all lawyers who love Scott, and their name is legion.

XX.

" SOUND, SOUND THE CLARION ! "

(1920.)

Sound, sound the clarion, fill the fife,
  To all
  Throughout } the sensual world proclaim
One crowded hour of glorious life
  Is worth an age without a name !

WHO wrote this magnificent stanza, that first attracted the world's attention in 1816, when it appeared as the motto to the fifth chapter of the fourth volume of the first series of " Tales of My Landlord " (" Old Mortality "), with " Anonymous " beneath it ? (In the collected edition it is the thirty-fourth chapter of " Old Mortality.") Hitherto no one of us has ever entertained a doubt.

Yet in 1920 Mr. James Rankin, of Galashiels, made the discovery that in October, 1791, in a copy of a " literary weekly " published in Edinburgh, and called the *Bee*, this very stanza appeared with thirteen others in " a poem said to have been written by Major Mordaunt during the last German War, never before published."

Mr. T. Craig Brown, of Selkirk, in an interesting letter that appeared in the *Literary Supplement* to *The Times*, has reprinted *all* the stanzas that make up this poem, and has supplied us with full particulars of Major Mordaunt's honourable life, which came to an end in St. James's Place, London, in 1809, in the eightieth year of his age. So far as is known, the major (who died a lieutenant-general) wrote no other poetry, good, bad, or indifferent.

It would be unkind to the memory of a gallant soldier to reprint again the other thirteen stanzas of this his sole known poetical effusion, although the stanza immediately preceding the one quoted by Scott in " Old Mortality " is not without some merit.   It runs as follows :

> But stop, my Chloe, wanton muse,
>   Indulge not this unmanly strain ;
> Beat, beat the drums, my ardour rouse,
>   And call the soldier back again !

On reading Mr. Craig's letter and Major Mordaunt's poem, I felt impelled to address the following letter to the Editor of the *Literary Supplement* :

"SIR,—Although the rediscovery of the Edinburgh *Bee* (1791) throws an uncomfortable doubt upon the Scott authorship of the glowing stanza in question, this much at least is certain (else literature is a lie), that whoever may have been its author, it was not the feckless composer of thirteen out of the fourteen verses you have been so good as to reprint in last Thursday's issue of your *Supplement.*

" In October, 1791, Scott was in Edinburgh reading for the Bar, aged twenty-one, and living in close intimacy with ' the lads of the Literary Society,' and was also secretary of the famous ' Speculative Society.' That he kept his eye upon the *Bee* and kindred adventures is certain. The editor was probably well known to him, and I, at all events, find it easy, in my mind's eye, to see Scott in the editor's room glancing over these vapid verses, attributed to Major Mordaunt, and, catching fire at the tenth stanza,

Beat, beat the drums, my ardour rouse,

sitting down, and, in a fine frenzy, dashing off the immortal lines that have reverberated through the world for nearly one hundred and thirty years. This is not ' proof positive,' but it is good enough for me.

" Scott's indifference to this question of author-

ship is well known, and an odd, half-forgotten
example of it may be worth mentioning. In 1822
Scott's publisher, Archibald Constable, printed a
pretty little volume called ' The Poetry contained
in the Novels, Tales and Romances of the Author
of " Waverley," wherein are collected all the
mottoes and scraps of poetry printed and quoted
in as many of the Waverley Novels as were then
in existence, and, amongst others, under ' Old
Mortality,' the stanza in question.

" The ' advertisement ' to this little book, which
is very much in Scott's ironical style, has the
following passage :

" We believe by far the greater part of the poetry inter-
spersed through these novels to be original compositions of the
author.   At the same time the reader will find passages which
are quoted by other authors, and very probably detect more
of them than our limited reading has enabled us to ascertain ;
indeed, it is our opinion that some of the following poetry is
neither entirely original nor altogether borrowed, but consists
in some instances of passages from other writers which the
author has not hesitated to alter considerably, either to supply
defects of his own memory or to adapt the quotations more
explicitly and aptly to the matter in hand.

" Who was the actual editor of this volume is not
known. It certainly was not Scott, who, although
he must have known of its existence, can never
have even glanced through its contents, for on

page 101 it contains, without a word of comment, Lovelace's stanza beginning

> Stone walls do not a prison make,

quoted in 'Old Mortality,' and on page 115 Bunyan's

> He that is down need fear no fall,

quoted by Madge Wildfire in 'The Heart of Midlothian.'

" It is curious to have to relate that when Moxon in 1866 issued, in his series of ' Miniature Poets,' ' A Selection from the Works of Scott,' whilst Lovelace was too much for the editor, Bunyan's verses, although to be read in the most widely circulated of British books, are to be found as an original production of Sir Walter's.

" A new edition of Constable's little book, taking in all the Waverley Novels (with a few judicious notes) would be a good thing.

" Yours truly.

"*August,* 1920."

XXI.

THE RADICAL TAILOR OF CHARING CROSS.*

(1919.)

THIS is a reprint, at a lower price, of Mr. Wallas's " Life of Francis Place," published by Longman's in 1898. It is an illuminating, interesting, and timely book, and one far better worth reading in these mysterious and clouded days than any of the Lives of the Prime Ministers, Lord Chancellors, and Archbishops who " flourished " during the same period. Mr. Wallas deserves to be congratulated again upon the skill he has exhibited in reducing to one volume of four hundred pages the most bewildering mass of manuscript material ever left behind, if not by mortal man, at all events by any previous maker of leather breeches.

The British Museum is a big building, and so, I doubt not, is its storehouse at Hendon, and in one

---

* " The Life of Francis Place (1771–1854)." By Graham Wallas. (Allen and Unwin.)

or other of these depositaries are to-day to be found the following " footprints " of Francis Place :

(1) An autobiography of such prodigious proportions that even a biographer of Mr. Wallas's sturdy build is found declaring that " it never was and never will be published," a rash thing to assert of any manuscript in these days.

(2) Many volumes of letter-books containing original letters to Place, with copies of his replies.

(3) Volumes of correspondence between Place and Byron's friend, Sir John Cam Hobhouse, afterwards Lord Broughton.

(4) Seventy volumes of unfinished manuscripts of intended books on subjects which Place had made his very own.

(5) One hundred and eighty volumes of newspaper cuttings, letters, and pamphlets, all concerned with matters of merely historical and social importance.

And there are more materials in the United States of America, whither, so Mr. Wallas says, in a fine flight of fancy, " some future historian " " may perhaps " have to follow them.

The admirable use, necessarily sparing, Mr. Wallas has been able to make of so much of this material as he knew about when he wrote his book,

will force upon the mind of a judicious reader the
conviction, however unwelcome, that, although it
would be absurd to allow these huge collections to
upset the whole balance of a student's short life,
yet that every one of these volumes probably contains matter highly relevant to the comprehension
of the toilsome labours of one of the clearest-
headed, most disinterested, as well as industrious
of men.

The early days of this honest reformer can only
be described as Hogarthian in their horror. " Gin
Lane " would appear to have been the nursing
mother of one of the most virtuous and efficient of
men.

He was born in a sponging house, or private
debtor's prison, in Vinegar Yard, Drury Lane,
kept by his father, who, in 1771, was a bailiff to
the Marshalsea Court. This father, who by trade
was a journeyman baker, was not a man of con-
ciliatory demeanour. " If he were coming along
a passage or any narrow place, such as a doorway,
and was met either by me or my brother, he always
made a blow at us with his fist for coming in his
way. If we attempted to retreat, he would make
us come forward, and, as certainly as we came
forward, he would knock us down." He was also

an inveterate gambler, and the home, if home it
can be called, was more than once broken up
owing to his losses in the State lotteries of the
time.

The young Francis, thus reared, took his full
share, so Mr. Wallas tells us from the autobiography, " in the now incredible street life which
flourished in London before the new police.   He
was skilled in street games, a hunter of bullocks
in the Strand, an obstinate faction-fighter, and a
daily witness of every form of open crime and
debauchery." When he grew a little older he
belonged to " a cutter club," an eight-oared boat's
crew, the coxswain of which was transported for a
robbery and the stroke oar hanged on a charge of
murder.   When Francis reached the age of fourteen his father was seized with one of the quaintest
of paternal notions, and told the boy he was forthwith to be apprenticed, not to a brazier, as Mr.
Dick wished David Copperfield to be, but, of all
things in the world, to a conveyancer ! and this
not in the Pistolian sense of the word.   But
Vinegar Yard had its proper sense of pride, and
the boy rebelled and swore that he would never be
a lawyer, but must have a regular " trade " ; and
thereupon his father, that very same evening, over

a pot of ale, apprenticed him to " a drunken little
wretch " who undertook to initiate him into the
art and mystery of a leather breeches maker, an
industry even then as decayed as the art of con-
veyancing has since become. And that is how
Francis Place, the friend of Mill, Bentham, Grote,
and Cobden, and as good a man as any of them,
became a tailor, and, what is more, made a fortune
in his trade. Strictly speaking, perhaps, Place
never was a tailor—for he never cut a coat, though
he employed those who cut Lord Melbourne's
coats—but he could make leather breeches against
any man in England.

What an education for a moralist and a reformer ! Where, I wonder, even in 1775, could
he have got a worse one ? But somehow or
another it did not turn out so very badly. From
four to fourteen Place went to school " in the
neighbourhood of Drury Lane," and " in his
twelfth year he came under a kindly, ineffectual
teacher who lent him books, gave him good advice,
and lectured him, with the other pupils, on the
elements of morality." Could Socrates have done
more ? Place, whose words may be taken, records
" that he could not recollect a single act of dis-
honesty during his apprenticeship," and, unless it

is a sin for a tailor to be occasionally a trifle overbearing and dictatorial, one cannot even hint at a
grave fault in the structure of his character. As
compared with the elder Mill, for example, he
shines with all the radiance of a star.

The poverty of Place's early life is too harrowing
to dwell upon. His father, who had become a
publican, sold his public-house and at once proceeded to lose all the purchase-money in a lottery.
His mother became a washerwoman. At the age
of nineteen Francis married a girl of seventeen and
went to live with her in one room in a court off
the Strand, on a weekly wage of just as many
shillings as his wife had years.

The horror of this " one room " situation was
Place's true political education, and coloured all
his thoughts, and occasionally imparts to his cool,
level-paced, pedestrian prose an apostolic glow and
fervour. Read what he is found writing on page
163 of the working man's craving for leisure :

> I know not how to describe the sickening aversion which at
> times steals over the working man and utterly disables him, for
> a longer or shorter period, from following his usual occupation,
> and compels him to indulge in *idleness*.

How Place emerged from this poverty and lived
to become one of the most powerful of London

citizens and the most useful of political reformers may be read in Mr. Wallas's book, which deserves to be put side by side with Mr. Hammond's " Town Labourer."

It is, happily, impossible in a short review to epitomise the energies of this indefatigable man. How Mr. Wallas has been able to do it within the compass of four hundred pages is a remarkable feat of authorship. One of Place's rules of action was " a man must have a good many projects in hand to accomplish any," and on page 186 Mr. Wallas records an astounding number of these projects, and it must always be remembered that in the Place vocabulary the word " project " meant something *he saw his way to do*. This tailor always cut his cloth with intent to clothe his man. He was a stern economist of his time, his labour, and his emotions. His " goose " was never a wild goose.

" The most striking piece of work Place ever carried through single-handed " was the repeal of the monstrous Combinations Laws in 1824–25.

To read Mr. Wallas's eighth chapter, which deals with this amazing subject, after laying down your morning's *Times* containing a verbatim report of the commission now sitting under the impartial chairmanship of a judge of the High Court, is to suffer so violent a change of mental atmosphere as to be risky for well-to-do invalids.

Place writes :

The cruel persecutions of the journeymen printers employed on *The Times* newspaper in 1810 were carried to an almost incredible extent.   The judge who tried them was the then Common Serjeant of London, Sir John Silvester, commonly known as "Bloody Black Jack."* . . . The men were sentenced, and *The Times* of two days afterwards contains the text of "Bloody Black Jack's" pronouncement.   "Prisoners, you have been convicted of a most wicked conspiracy to injure the most vital interests of those very employers who gave you bread, with intent to impede and injure them in their business, and, indeed, as far as in you lay, to effect their ruin.   The frequency of such crimes among men of your class of life and their mischievous and dangerous tendency to ruin the fortunes of those employers, which a principle of gratitude and self-interest should induce you to support, demand of the law that a severe example should be made of those persons who shall be convicted of such daring and flagitious combinations in defiance of public justice and in violation of public order.   No symptom of contrition has appeared."

After this preachment the sentences followed, varying from nine months to two years.

If it be urged that 1810 is almost as "far off and long ago " as the reign of King Richard II., it may be said, in the first place, that down to our own time the language of the civil magistrate in such cases was not very different from that of " Bloody Black Jack," who, I have no doubt, was a Bencher

* For a horrible story of this Common Serjeant see Jerdan's Autobiography 1—p. 121.

of his Inn ; and, in the second place, if it is different to-day, a large measure of praise is due to the man who, born in Vinegar Yard, scorned to be a lawyer, and dared to be a tailor.

Though Place was terribly enmeshed in the political business of his own hour, and was not, by the order of his mind, a prophet or even a philosopher, none the less his correspondence is occasionally illuminated by flashes of insight you may look for in vain in the letters of the " great men " who thought they were the " natural leaders " of a nascent democracy. Take education, for example. The Chartists, on whom Place gazed with a smile that must have been irritating, thought some of their funds might be advantageously expended in building schools all over the country. " But," writes Place, who was a great believer in the cold water cure, and threw it with both hands :

I am certain you will never have even one school. You will never raise £3,000 for such a purpose, and £3,000 would not pay for such a school as you have described. I hope to see the time when £20,000,000 will be voted to pay for the building of schools—schools for all, and not schools for Churchmen or Chartists only, and when a compulsory rate will be levied on all, in each school district by a committee of the district, to pay the expenses of carrying on the schools, in which the teaching shall be really good, and apart from all religion, and especially from all sectarianism, whether religious or political.

Long after the date of this letter Place died,

worn out, in 1854, sixteen years before the first Education Act worthy of the name and the nation.

I have already referred to Place's habit of throwing cold water on hasty schemes involving the expenditure of scanty funds. There was a Chartist leader, famous in his day in some quarters and infamous in others, Henry Vincent, a good fellow, but gaseous, much addicted to rhetoric, and a shocking bad man of business. He wanted to get into Parliament for Banbury, where he was told, and believed, his return " was certain." He wrote to Place inviting pecuniary assistance. Place's reply may be read in Mr. Wallas, but not here. To put it mildly, Place advised Vincent to leave Banbury, with its three hundred electors, severely alone. His advice was, of course, not taken, and Vincent polled fifty-one votes out of the three hundred. This happened in 1841. In 1842 Vincent was beaten at Ipswich. In 1843 at Tavistock. In 1844 at Kilmarnock. In 1846 at Plymouth. In 1847 and 1848 again and again at Ipswich. In 1852 at York. Vincent never got in anywhere at any time, and it was, perhaps, fortunate for the House of Commons he did not, for, in the opinion of many bad judges, he was

" the most eloquent man of his time." If, however, Vincent was glad when he heard of Place's
death in 1854, not only do I find it easy to forgive
him, but so will you if you read Place's letter
to him.

Place knew both the elder and the younger
Mill, and his humanity was evidently not a little
shocked by the painful spectacle which he once
witnessed at Bentham's country house of the elder
Mill " cuffing and scolding " his crying children
over their preposterous lessons, which began every
morning at the inhuman hour of six. And yet
Place had known a father who knocked his son
down whenever he saw him.

The elder Place or the elder Mill, which father
was the more harmful ?   I think I know—but dare
not say.   " Oh, mystery of mysteries !   Education,
what art thou ? "

It is, perhaps, only fair to add, in concluding,
that Place was not only a tailor, but also an
agnostic, an anti-Socialist, and (though he had
himself fifteen children) a neo-Malthusian !

XXII.

ARTHUR HALL, M.P. FOR GRANTHAM.

(1919.)

My advice to any one who wishes to enjoy as
it ought to be enjoyed this excellent biography *
is resolutely to forget (if he ever knew) the fact
that its subject, an extravagant and unfortunate
Elizabethan, was the first, and the worst, English
translator of the " Iliad " of Homer.

But why should I thus early do Hall this injustice, for he never attempted, and never even
professed, to translate Homer ? To say that Hall
knew less Greek than Pope would be to indulge
an unworthy sneer, for Hall knew no Greek, and
only enough Latin to enable him to quote a
familiar tag or two from the " Æneid." Hall made
no use of the Latin translations of the " Iliad "
then in print, but from the beginning to the end

* " The Life and Works of Arthur Hall, of Grantham, M.P.,
Courtier, and First Translator of Homer into English." By
H. G. Wright, M.A. (Manchester : at the University Press.
Longmans, 1919.)

of his enterprise worked steadily away upon the French version of M. Hugues Salel, the second edition of which was printed in Paris in 1555. The very copy of Salel used by Hall is now, bearing marks of ill usage, in the British Museum. Hall was, at all events, an honest man and did not attempt, as other translators have done, to cover up his ignorance, for the title page of his quarto runs as follows :

Ten Books of Homer's "Iliad," translated out of the French by Arthur Hall, Esquire, at London. Imprinted by Ralph Newberie, 1581. *Cum privilegio.*

Consequently, Hall's " Homer's ' Iliad ' " is not Homer's " Iliad " (which, as Shirley Brooks once truly said, " is still the best "), but Salel's " Homer's ' Iliad,' " worsened by Hall. To forget as speedily as possible all about such an outrage is a duty owing to oneself no less than to the " injur'd shade " of the Father of Poetry.

Mr. Wright, Hall's biographer, though candid and outspoken upon the demerits of this version, does not cold-shoulder it as much as he might well have done, but devotes his four last chapters to its consideration ; and this although the best things he can find to say about it are that Shakespeare *might* have read it (though I will wager my

only " quarto " that he never did), and that the
very badness of Hall's translation *may* have
suggested to the fertile brain of Chapman both the
propriety and the ease of making a better one.

If this is the most an honest and learned
biographer can find to say, I, who am not Hall's
biographer or the owner of any of the only five
copies now known to exist of the original edition
of 1581 (and only one poor reprint has ever since
been asked for), may be pardoned if I give
Messieurs Salel and Hall the go-by and devote my
exclusive attention to the really interesting things
about Arthur Hall—viz., his own life and curious
adventures.

The first unusual thing about the old-time M.P.
for Grantham is that, though in all his bones a
litigious, wrong-headed, self-assertive John Bull,
he was a Calais man born and bred. Englishmen
have still so many possessions outside Britain that
they can always find it easy to forget how they
acquired them and when they lost any of them.
How many of us remember that Java was once
ours for five glorious years ? And as for Calais,
but for the story which, happily, has found its
way into those chief sources of an Englishman's
historical knowledge, children's lesson books,

about Mary Tudor's distress when she heard of the capture of Calais, we might have forgotten for how many years Calais was directly represented in the English House of Commons.

Yet it is well that we should occasionally remember that Calais was once an English town, since we must at the same time be reminded that but for the combined valour of English and French soldiers it might at this moment be a German town.

How Arthur Hall came to be born in Calais in 1539 is explained by Mr. Wright in his early chapters. Arthur's great-grandfather, Thomas Hall, was a wealthy merchant of Grantham, and landed proprietor in Lincolnshire, who was chosen to entertain in 1503 the Lady Margaret Tudor, on her way to Scotland to marry King James IV., who fell at Flodden. Thomas Hall was a merchant of the Staple of Calais, and his grandson Francis, the father of Arthur, led a life described by Mr. Wright as bound up with "the old Fortress," and who, when he came to die in 1532, after many strange Continental adventures, both warlike and diplomatic, was styled "Comptroller of the King's Majesty's Towne and Marches of Calais."

The King's representatives in Calais were called "deputy," and they succeeded one another as rapidly as do Irish Lord Lieutenants in the present day. Sir Robert Wingfield, Lord Berners, Lord Lisle, Lord Maltravers, and Lord Cobham all filled this high office in Francis Hall's time.

Arthur Hall spent the first thirteen years of his life—and they were probably his happiest years—in Calais, amid sights, sounds, and surroundings vividly described in Mr. Wright's pages.

The next interesting thing about Arthur Hall is the fact that on his father's death he became the ward of Sir William Cecil, afterwards Lord Burghley. Great men in those days sought after profitable wardships as in later times after directorships, and as Hall had succeeded not only to lands in France and a well-furnished house in Calais, but to the patrimonial acres in Lincolnshire, Cecil's own county, his guardianship extended Cecil's local interest and put a little then much-needed money in his pocket. It certainly added to his many burdens, for his ward, despite his veneration for his guardian, was a very troublesome fellow, a hardened grumbler, and all his life an indefatigable and tiresome correspondent. His mother, Ursula Hall, who was left behind in Calais, was loth to part with her only son, but in those unfeeling Tudor days mothers' tears counted for nothing, and the young Arthur was despatched, in 1552, across the Channel to become a member of Cecil's household and the companion of his eldest son, to whom in after years he dedicated his French Homer.

Mr. Wright gives a pleasing account of the Cecil *menage*, which fully supports the delightful testimony given by Roger Ascham in his Preface to that noble book " The Scholemaster." Ascham and the youthful Hall became friends, or at least acquaintances, and on one occasion, when walking together some eighteen or nineteen years before 1581, Ascham, on hearing from his youthful companion that the latter had already begun to turn Homer into English, "animated him with great entreatie to go forward with his begun enterprise." Whether Hall had the courage to tell Ascham that he did not know any Greek and derived his knowledge of Homer from a French version may be doubted.

Sir William Cecil's household was, if not a nest of singing birds, at all events the abode of translators who dedicated their productions to their great patron. These useful labourers in the fields of literature were usually either Lincolnshire or Cambridge men.

Whether Hall was sent to Cambridge, Cecil's own University, cannot be proved. Mr. Wright thinks he was not, and attaches importance to the fact that in after years, when Hall was denouncing men who enter the House of Commons merely for their own advancement, he writes of one of these strange creatures as follows :

He had been, forsooth, perhaps at Cambridge and learned the fragments of a little sophistry, wherewith he, with his glossing tongue and studied words, may move many well-meaning gentlemen, who, for want of deep judgment, may say " Yea " to their own prejudice.

Mr. Wright, after quoting these words, adds romantically: " This is hardly the tone a man would use in referring to his *Alma Mater*, and confirms the opinion that Hall was never at St. John's College, Cambridge."

Though commending, I cannot share this opinion, for I have myself known one or two Cambridge men in the House of Commons who have answered so closely to Hall's description as to compel me to overlook the slight it casts upon my own University in consideration of the force and justice of the criticism.

The next interesting thing about Hall is that he

was a considerable traveller. Some modern M.P.'s have been known to confide to the compiler of that model of terse biography, "Dod's Parliamentary Companion," the fact that they have travelled "extensively." The Member for Grantham, considering his day, may be said to have travelled extensively, for not only was he abroad, mainly in Italy, for two years (1567–1569), but he reached Constantinople, where, as Mr. Wright puts it, "he rubbed shoulders with the Turk, and felt the glamour of the East." Whilst abroad he corresponded regularly with Sir William Cecil, and interesting records of his travels may be read both in the biography and in the appendix.

With Hall's entrance into the House of Commons as Member for Grantham, in April, 1571, his public troubles began. The contemporary proverb, "*Inglese italinato e un diavolo incarnato,*" is, at all events, illustrated by the story of Hall's later days. His troubles began almost at once, for in May, 1572, he was brought to the bar of the House in custody of the Serjeant, on the charge of having made "sundry lewd speeches as well in the House and abroad." Faced by Mr. Speaker, he confessed his folly, apologised, and, after receiving a reprimand from the Chair, was discharged. It is only fair to add that on this occasion the violence of his language was attributable to his zeal for Mary Queen of Scots.   His subsequent quarrels have no such romantic excuse.

His next most famous quarrel, narrated at great length by Mr. Wright, whose interest in such affairs never flags, reveals this first and worst translator of the " Iliad " in a lamentable light as a tavern-haunter, dicer, and street brawler.   His enemy rejoiced in the name of Melchisedech Mallory.   The tale is too long to retell in this place.   It raised a nice question of parliamentary privilege, and, indeed, in that curious branch of the law Hall must be ranked with Wilkes, for on another occasion of breach of privilege—viz., the publication by Hall of a once-notorious letter (without a printer's name) slandering some of his brother M.P.'s, and, what was worse, " impeaching the memory of the late Speaker "—he was not only sent to the Tower, but by resolution expelled from the House ; and a new writ was forthwith issued for Grantham, and Hall's successor was allowed to take his seat without protest or demur.   These are, indeed, high matters, and are fitly recorded in Hatsell's Precedents.

But, though Hall's quarrels were endless, there

must be an end to this review, and consequently only one more can be referred to—his quarrel with a widow of high degree. The details are, perhaps, a little delicate, and as Mr. Wright sets them out in full detail (pages 76–77) I need add no remarks of my own beyond mentioning the lady's name. It was the Lady Sidney Sussex, the pious foundress of the college at Cambridge. " Sidney Sussex " is famous in the history of the University for having once sheltered two undergraduates—the one Oliver Cromwell, a former Lord High Protector of these realms ; the other of a later date, who, having insisted " that W plus X was the same as XW," was harshly challenged by the authorities as follows : " Sir, we must trouble you to confine that idea to Sid. Sussex," and, feeling unable " to see the matter through," took (such at least was the common report) to his bed and died.

The most melancholy event in Hall's life (which ended in 1605) now falls to be recorded. Sunday, November 24th, 1588, was spent by him in the Fleet Prison. " What of that ? " do you callously inquire ? Have you, then, indeed forgotten that November 24th, 1588 (a Sunday), was the very day Queen Elizabeth, attended by her Court and her Privy Council, drove down to St. Paul's in a coach drawn by four white horses, to return thanks to Almighty God for the defeat of the Spanish Armada ?

One of the three or four really great days in English history ! And Arthur Hall, a true, if quarrelsome, patriot, spent it in the Fleet. Thus was the Father of Poetry avenged.

XXIII.

CHATEAUBRIAND.*

(*The Westminster Gazette*, 1902.)

THERE are names in literature which never
cease to sound in the ear with something of the
mystery of the waves lapping the shore, or of the
wind among the boughs. Such a name is Chateaubriand's—such a name Carlyle's may some day
become. There are authors you cannot get rid of
by the easy expedient of ceasing to read their
books, for they have made their way into the
national life and remain embedded in the structure
of things. In FitzGerald's phrase, they make
" peat."

The days when " Atala," " René," and " Le
Génie du Christianisme " were read by all young
and ingenuous souls in France and, through translations, in Spain, Italy, Germany, and England,
are gone, never to return ; for it would be as easy

* " The Memoirs of François René, Vicomte de Chateaubriand, sometime Ambassador to England." Translated by
A. T. de Mattos. In six volumes. (Freemantle & Co.)

to recall Louis XVIII. from his grave as the environment that made " Atala " a well-spring of passion, " René " a fount of devotion, and " Le Génie " an arc in the heavens. But their author remains—a great name still sounding in the ear.

Chateaubriand was born in Napoleon's year (1768), and died in 1848, that period of ignoble revolutions. He belonged to the *noblesse*, and his account of his childhood and early manhood in St. Malo and the chateau of Combourg, though possibly somewhat accentuated, is wonderful writing, and gives an impression of *ennui*, *tristesse*, and wasted time quite ineffaceable.

Supper over, the four of us would leave the table and gather round the chimney. My mother flung herself with a sigh upon an old couch covered with imitation Siam : a stand was put before her with a candle. I sat down with Lucile by the fire, the servants cleared the table and withdrew. My father then began a tramp which lasted till he went to bed. He was dressed in a white rateen gown, a kind of cloak which I have seen no one wear except him. His half-bald head was covered with a big white cap that stood straight up on end. When he walked away to a distance from the fireplace the huge hall was so badly lighted by its solitary candle that he was no longer visible ; we could only hear him still walking in the darkness ; then he would slowly return towards the light and gradually emerge from the dusk, like a ghost with his white gown, his white cap, his long, pale face. Lucile and I exchanged a few words in a low voice when he was at the other end of the hall. We hushed when he drew nearer to us. . . . The hour of ten struck on the castle clock. My father stopped. He drew out his watch, wound it, took a great silver candlestick holding a

tall candle, and went towards his bedroom, which formed part
of the East Tower. Lucile and I placed ourselves on his way,
kissed him, and bade him good-night. He turned his dry,
hollow cheek to us without replying, continued his road, withdrew inside the tower, the doors of which we heard closing
behind him.

A notable addition to the Gallery of Fathers !
In the Terror the chateau became a prison, but it
can hardly have been a less lively place than it
was in the time of the high and mighty René de
Chateaubriand, Count of Combourg, Lord of
Gangres, etc.

Combourg did not escape the quick eye of that
famous finger-post to the Revolution, our own
Arthur Young, who thus describes it :

To Combourg the country has a savage aspect, husbandry
has not much further advanced than among the Hurons, the
people almost as wild as their country, and their town of Combourg, one of the most brutal filthy places that can be seen ;
mud houses, no windows, and pavements so broken as to
impede all passengers. Yet here is a chateau, and inhabited !
Who is this Monsieur de Chateaubriand, the owner, that has
nerves strung for a residence amidst such filth and poverty ?

When Arthur Young passed through Combourg
on September 1st, 1788, the old lord of the rateen
gown had been dead two years, and the Monsieur
de Chateaubriand he invokes was our author's
elder brother, who was destined to be carried to
the guillotine in the Place de la Révolution, in the

company of his wife and of the aged Malesherbes, on the 22nd Floreal, Year II. of the French Republic.

In the first two volumes of M. de Mattos' admirable translation we can read of Louis XVI. out hunting ; of the fall of the Bastille, which Chateaubriand witnessed ; of speeches by Mirabeau and Robespierre in the Constituent Assembly, which he heard ; of plays and dinnerparties, and heads on pikes. Suddenly the scene shifts : Chateaubriand, who was then halting between two opinions, deserts his country and the growing horrors of Paris and crosses the seas, bent on discovering the north-west passage to the Pole ; he arrives at Baltimore, where he dines with George Washington and half a dozen other guests, into whose too sympathetic ears he pours his tale of the Bastille. Meeting a sensible man bearing the sensible name of Swift, he abandons the Pole and wanders among forests and prairies, making ready friendship with Indian damsels and divining the secrets of Nature. Chateaubriand's is perhaps the first picturesque pen to describe Niagara. An English newspaper finds him among the Blue Mountains, thinking how happy he could be with his head laid upon the knees of a " sad "

Indian woman, but when he reads of the flight of the King and his arrest at Varennes, he comes straight home. He gets married, is reduced to poverty, and in 1793 arrives, alone, in England; inhabits a garret in Holborn, spends a night in Westminster Abbey curled up by Chatham's tomb; wanders in all our parks and pleasant places, and even finds his way to Bungay, where he forgets to tell the daughter of the clergyman in whose house he is living that he has a wife in France.

In 1800 " Atala," a religious romance of the Indian forest, appears on the crest of a wave of rising emotions. " Its principal characters," says George Brandes, " were soon to be seen adorning the walls of French inns in coloured prints, whilst their waxen images were sold on the quays of Paris with those of Christ and the Virgin." In 1802 came " Le Génie du Christianisme," and the same number of *Le Moniteur* that announced the Peace of Amiens and the Concordat with the Church contained an article by Fontanes on the book which, if Sainte Beuve is to be believed, introduced to the world the literature of the nineteenth century. " Le Génie " was taken to be the reconciliation of God and France. Sainte Beuve has told at length the story of the conversion of

Chateaubriand. Napoleon was never converted, but sentiment he ever loved, and the author of " Atala " and " Le Génie " soon found himself established at the Roman Legation. The murder of the Duc d'Enghien put an end to friendly relations between these two great men, though Bonaparte, on the death of Chenier, wished to see Chateaubriand fill the vacant chair in the Academy ; but to praise a Jacobin was more than Chateaubriand could manage. As time went on the dream of a restored monarchy took possession of his pen, and his tractate " Bonaparte and the Bourbons " was declared by Louis XVIII. to be worth more than an army.

After the Restoration Chateaubriand became a politician, occupying for a while the post of Minister of Foreign Affairs. In 1822 he came to England as French Ambassador.

His latter days were melancholy and devoured by *ennui*, despite the charm of Madame de Récamier's devotion and the *rus in urbe* of the " Abbaye aux Bois," where, surrounded by sympathetic friends, he would read aloud, or permit to be read, the most moving passages of his own memoirs.

Englishmen have never greatly taken to

Chateaubriand, and it is not to be supposed
they ever will. We have our own rhetoricians.
Chateaubriand cannot claim to belong to the first
rank of writers. He is neither a Rousseau nor a
Bossuet. His eloquence is not convincing, his
religion is not persuasive. He had not enough of
anything to make him happy. Even his egotism
is not sublime. He tells us more than once he can
believe in nothing except religion, but that is impossible ; and Chateaubriand's constitutional
scepticism included religion, let him protest as
loudly as he may. He who reads " Atala " to-day
cannot fail to perceive that it is not a religious
book, but one breathing a spirit every bit as much
standing in need of exorcism as anything that
proceeded from the humaner pen of Voltaire.

The years fly by, and it is startling to think that
it is well-nigh forty years since the " Essays on
Criticism " were first published, in one of which
Mr. Arnold took occasion to speak up on behalf of
Chateaubriand, and added these words : " One
production of his—' René '—is akin to the most
powerful productions of Byron—to the 'Childe
Harold ' or ' Manfred ' ; equal to them in power,
superior to them in form. But this work, I
hardly know why, is almost unread in England."

" René," I cannot but feel, is still less likely to be read in the England of 1902 than it was in the already distant days of 1865 ; but memoirs abound and are greatly in favour. Quite apart from his greatness as an author, and notwithstanding his devouring sense of his own importance, Chateaubriand had a keen interest in the men he met, and records with the true zest of a memoir writer the details of his eventful life. He did not like missing a sight, even going so far as to regret that, owing to temporary indisposition, he did not see Talleyrand say Mass in the Champ de Mars on July 14th, 1790. To us Londoners these Memoirs are particularly interesting, for their author is one of the shadows who still haunt Kensington Gardens, for there it was the poor emigrant devised the loves of " Atala " and jotted down in pencil the passions of René.

There are many illuminating passages and striking pages in the " Mémoires d'Outre-Tombe " which, once read, for ever haunt the memory and make a picture gallery of historic scenes and astounding events. It is not often that a poet, a rhetorician, a sentimentalist, and a politician finds himself so near the centre of things as was the author of " Les Martyrs " and " De Bonaparte et des Bourbons." Chateaubriand's sensitive spirit quivered and shook in every wind that produced both the Revolution and the Restoration in France.

Among these illuminating passages a great place must be given to those in the third part of the " Memoirs " (Volume III. of M. De Mattos, translation), in which he describes the entry into Paris of the allied armies on March 31st, 1814, " at midday, ten days only after the anniversary of the death of the Duc d'Enghien on March 21st, 1804."

Never were two events more unlike than the invasion of 1814 and that of 1815. In 1814 the armies of the Allies approached Paris in a positively sentimental spirit, and their proclamation was worthy of the nation to whose capital it was addressed :

Parisians, you know the situation in which your country is placed ; the preservation and the tranquillity of your city will be the object of the cares of the Allies. It is with these sentiments that Europe in arms before your walls addresses herself to you.

Chateaubriand, after quoting this proclamation, adds the comment : " What a magnificent acknowledgment of France's greatness ! " Before this trumpet-blast Jericho fell—" nobody, except the soldiers, wanted any more of Bonaparte, and, dreading lest they should keep him, the people hastened to open the gates " to let in Alexander, Czar of Russia, and the King of Prussia! What an anti-climax after all this waste of wealth and loss of blood!

Order, peace, and moderation reigned on every hand—the shops were reopened; Russian guardsmen, six feet tall, were piloted through the streets by little French rogues, who make fun of them as of jumping-jacks and carnival-maskers. The conquered might be taken for the conquerors; the latter, trembling at their successes, looked as though they were excusing themselves. . . . After five-and-twenty years the clash of arms ceased from one end of Europe to another.

Quite a love feast, and yet Chateaubriand was not happy when he saw Alexander of Russia and the Prussian king ride into Paris :

I saw them defile along the boulevards. Feeling stupefied and dumbfounded within myself, as though my name as a Frenchman had been torn from me to substitute for it the name by which I was thenceforth to be known in the mines of Siberia, I felt, at the same time, my exasperation increase against the man whose glory had reduced us to that disgrace.

Where, meanwhile, was the " Man of Glory," the " Victor of Borodino " ? He had capitulated at Fontainebleau and ordered his Austrian wife and the King of Rome to leave Paris, which he placed under the charge of the ex-King of Spain, who plastered its walls with the following majestic proclamation :

King Joseph, Lieutenant-General of the Empire, Commander-in-Chief of the National Guard. Citizens of Paris.

The Court of Regency has provided for the safety of the Empress and the King of Rome. *I remain with you.* Let us arm ourselves to defend this town, its monuments, its riches, our wives, our children, all that is dear to us. Let this vast city become a camp for a short while, that the enemy meet with his disgrace under its walls, which he hopes to surmount in triumph.

Having given this honest employment to the printers and billstickers of Paris, " King Joseph " absconded to Blois, whence he made his way to Switzerland. His criticism of his distinguished relative was an odd one. " I should not," said he, " call my brother so much a great man as a good one ! "

Bonaparte himself retired behind the Loire, accompanied by some 40,000 picked soldiers. The times remained critical. Who was to come back to the Tuileries, which the Czar had refused to inhabit, remembering, says Chateaubriand, how Bonaparte had lolled in the palaces of Vienna, Berlin, and Moscow ? Talleyrand favoured a Regency, with the young King of Rome as the future sovereign, but Chateaubriand, though with a sad heart, for he well knew the limitations of the breed, for whom, indeed, his contempt keeps cropping up in scores of bitter sentences, espoused the cause of the old family. We cannot but smile at the vanity of the author who records the genesis of his pamphlet, " De Bonaparte et des Bourbons," with as much emphasis as if it were an entry into Paris, but pamphlets before now have played great parts, and Louis XVIII. at all events, as before mentioned, declared that Chateaubriand's pamphlet was worth more than an army of a hundred thousand men. Even this extravagant praise did not satisfy an author's vanity, for, after repeating it, Chateaubriand adds, " He (Louis) might have said it was a certificate of existence to him."

It was in those critical days that I threw down my pamphlet to turn the scale—its result is well known. I flung myself headlong into the fray to serve as a shield to liberty. I spoke in the name of the Legitimacy in order to add to my words the authority of positive affairs. I taught France what the old Royal Family was. I told her how many members of that family existed, what their names were and their character ; it was as though I had drawn up a list of the children of the Emperor of China, to so great an extent had the Republic and the Empire encroached upon the present and relegated the Bourbons to the past.

It was the misfortune of Chateaubriand to be the evangel of a worn-out creed. He had no belief in Louis XVIII. Back the Bourbons came, having learnt nothing and forgotten nothing, full of their fatuous egotism, solitary believers in their own rights and titles. Chateaubriand, who knew everybody, was only able to count upon his fingers eight avowed Royalists on aristocratic principles among the motley and hypocritical crowd who pulled down the statue of their late tyrant from the column in the Place Vendôme. The majority, so he emphatically declares, was not a Legitimist one—it was the men of the Republic and the Empire who greeted with enthusiasm the Restoration—nor was the tale of their perfidies and perjuries yet fully told. It was a hideous spectacle. With what furious eloquence does Chateaubriand describe it :

The Ministers, the high dignitaries, vied with each other in taking the oath to the Legitimacy ; all the civil and judicial authorities crowded on each other's heels to swear hatred against the proscribed new dynasty, and love to the ancient race whom they had a hundred and a hundred times condemned. Who drew up those proclamations, those adulatory addresses, so insulting to Napoleon, with which France was flooded ? The Royalists ? No—the Ministers, the generals, the authorities chosen and maintained in office by Bonaparte. Where was the jobbing of the Restoration done ? At the Royalists' ? No. At M. de Talleyrand's. With whom ? With M. de Pradt, almoner to the God Mars, and mitred mountebank. Where were entertainments given to the "infamous foreign Princes" ? At the country houses of the Royalists ? No—at Malmaison. To whom did Napoleon's dearest friends—Berthier, for example—carry their ardent devotion ? To the Legitimacy. Who spent their existences with the Emperor Alexander, with that "brutal Tartar" ? The classes of the Institute, the scholars, the men of letters, the philosophers, philanthropists, theophilanthropists, and others ; they returned enchanted, laden with praises and snuff boxes.

How often has Milton's line come to our relief and helped us to give expression to our emotions :

Owls and cuckoos, asses, apes, and dogs ;

though I think our blind Maeonides owes an apology to what finer writers call the " canine species " for including them in his catalogue ; but rhyme has its exigencies.

Nor is any relief to be found from this sordid exhibition of meanness and vulgar delusion by turning away from Paris to contemplate the actions of the " Man of Destiny " whilst being personally conducted by the commissaries of the Allies to the island of Elba, protected by foreign hands against his own people. Count Waldburg's " Itinerary of Napoleon from Fontainebleau to Elba " is a terrible tract, and belittles Napoleon the Great even more effectually than Hugo was able to do Napoleon the Small :

The hero, reduced to tears and disguises, weeping under a post-boy's jacket in the corner of an inn. . . . The master of the nations encouraging the Commissaries to heap humiliations upon him in order that he might escape detection ; delighted to have General Koller whistling in his presence, and a coachman puffing smoke in his face ; compelling General Schouvaloff's aide-de-camp, to play the part of the Emperor, whilst he,

Bonaparte, wore the dress of an Austrian colonel and covered himself up in the cloak of a Russian general.

And all this because a man who had sent millions of his fellow creatures to Hades before their day was himself afraid to die! Yet, so puzzling is human nature, this cowering creature was still to be the Hero of the Hundred Days, and to drive once more before him, like withered leaves before the wind, the restored monarch of the ancient line and as many of his courtiers as did not run back to wear the Imperial livery.

The next time "Divine Right" returned to Paris Waterloo had been fought and Louis XVIII. had Wellington by his side to tell him what to do and what Ministers to choose.

Thereon hangs a tale which Chateaubriand tells. Wellington was firm that Fouché should be a Minister of the Crown—Fouché, whose hands were red with royal blood, and who was more of a regicide than Cromwell himself! This was pointed out to the Duke, and what was his reply? "Oh, that's a trifle!"

I congratulate Mr. de Mattos on a completed work. He has finished and seen published in six volumes his translation of a famous book, and is able to record the wish that he could have been as long over the translation as was the author over the composition—thirty years — for then, says he, " I should have known scarce a dull moment." So fine a compliment, so well bestowed, would have given great pleasure to M. le Vicomte de Chateaubriand.

It is a bearish thing to seek to get behind a compliment, and I hesitate to ask Mr. de Mattos, who, from his few notes and explanatory remarks, I judge to be both a pious Catholic and a good Legitimist, whether, when his important and lengthy task was done, and for the last time he pushed aside his pen and rose from the table, for ever quit of Chateaubriand, he felt satisfied in his own mind as to the Catholicism and Legitimism of the man in whose company he had spent so much time. But no one is entitled to ask such questions of a stranger.

The two concluding volumes which have just appeared, though of necessity lacking the terrible interest of the first two, which tell of the Revolution and the Terror, or the fascination of the second two volumes, which show Chateaubriand struggling between his hatred of Napoleon and his innate love of " glory," are yet full of sap and meat for those curious readers who love to pry into the

motives of men and allow themselves time to feel
the pulses of humanity, and are therefore as much
interested in the fantasies of a king in exile, living
in a borrowed castle, nursing " a principle," and
receiving the homage of a handful of battered
courtiers, themselves divided into hostile parties
and much given to intrigue, as in the pomp and
power of Louis Quatorze or the plots and plans of
Richelieu or Mazarin.

As for Chateaubriand himself, his amazing
vanities and age-proof coxcombry enliven, but
cannot obscure, his keen insight into character and
the course of events. He was never befooled or
induced to take to his breast a single delusion.
Beneath his sentiment and " bursts of eloquence "
there is always a real grasp of the situation—a
grasp, however, which the reader cannot but feel
lacks the strength which alone enables a man not
merely to understand a situation, but to control it.
Chateaubriand sometimes affects to be unable to
comprehend why he was not able to save his
country on any of the too numerous occasions she
required that service. He was, he often reminds
his readers, a man of affairs, a most travelled
thane, a Foreign Minister, an ambassador, an
orator, and an aristocrat who was at once alive to

the sovereignty of the people, the greatness of France, the freedom of the Press, the charm of religion, and the sanctity of the monarchical idea. Yet at the bottom of his heart Chateaubriand knew perfectly well that he could no more rule France than he could have written one of Molière's comedies. He was well qualified to play many parts, but he had nothing of the soldier in his composition, and was far happier scribbling his memoirs in a travelling-carriage than ever he would have been on a field of battle. Yet, though not strong enough to make a bid on his own behalf, he was too proud or too vain to conceal himself in another's gaberdine, though the robe was royal, or even to keep himself in the background and humour the ridiculous pride of the Bourbons. He had to feed too much vanity of his own to be able to spare any provender for his royal masters, who always felt uneasy in his august presence, and were glad when he had retreated backwards from their company.

It is sometimes difficult to resist the disagreeable conviction taking possession of you that both Chateaubriand's religion and loyalty arose from the sense of his own weakness rather than from personal love and devotion. Had he felt himself strong enough to stand alone he might have given both his God and his king the slip.

The charm of these Memoirs consists in their enabling you to lie back in your chair and watch the phantoms they describe defile through the dream of life. This fine phrase, I hasten to add, is Chateaubriand's own. " I have seen," he says, " so many phantoms defile through the dream of life." And so, indeed, he had. With what ghosts had he not conversed ? What speeches he had heard, what revolutions and changes of fortune he had witnessed and experienced ! As for the oaths he had heard men take, they leave our old friend the Vicar of Bray far, far behind. There are men who, " after taking the Oath to the Republic, one and indivisible, to the Directory of five persons, to the Consulate of three, to the Empire of one alone, to the First Restoration, to the Additional Act to the Constitutions of the Empire, to the Second Restoration, have something left to swear to Louis Philippe ; I am not so rich."

From the man with the head shaped like a pear, from the Philip of the *juste-milieu,* who pilfered " the Crown from the King and liberty from the people," Chateaubriand, though no believer in the future of Henri Cinq, held himself aloof and counted himself lucky to be able to get from a Jew no less a sum than seven hundred francs for the gold lace, tassels, bullioned fringe, and epaulettes appertaining to his robes as a peer of France. He died on July 4th, 1848 ; but months before that date he had fallen into a sort of speechless stupor, but whilst in this condition he heard, says Alexis de Tocqueville, "a rumour of the Revolution of February," and was told that Louis Philippe's Government had been overthrown. "He said, 'Well done,' and nothing more." Four months later, "the din of the days of June reached his ears, and again he asked what that noise was. They answered that people were fighting in Paris, and that it was the sound of cannon. Thereupon he made vain efforts to rise, saying, 'I want to go to it,' and was then silent, this time for ever ; for he died the next day."

"Brittany and Religion," says the translator in a short and interesting Appendix,

gave the author of the " Génie du Christianisme " a magnificent funeral. For half a century he has slept beside the waves, in his granite sepulchre under a stone, surrounded by a Gothic iron railing, and surmounted by a cross. For the rest, no inscription, no name, no date. He had asked that this might be so in his letter of 1831 to the Mayor of St. Malo. "The cross," he wrote, "will tell that the man resting at its feet was a Christian; that will be enough for my memory."

But when Chateaubriand wrote like this to the Mayor of St. Malo he had for the moment forgotten the Memoirs he had been writing all his life, which might be trusted to supply the remarkable deficiencies of the romantic tombstone so many travellers have gazed upon with emotion, all of them well knowing whose mortal remains lie beneath it.

These last volumes contain accounts of many interesting things, "*Choses vues*," to use the phrase of a greater than Chateaubriand. In 1829 Pope Leo XII. died, and, as the custom was, the ambassadors went to compliment the Congregation of Cardinals before these latter dignitaries were imprisoned in conclave. Chateaubriand was French Ambassador, and he tells us with greater spirit than piety the story of the election of Pius VIII., an amiable pontiff, who filled St. Peter's Chair but twenty months.

Chateaubriand, who was a great giver of feasts when in funds, entertained the whole conclave to dinner, and, what pleased him less, had to put up the French cardinals who came to attend it. The author of " Atala " and " René " had a business side to his character. He writes in the following strain to Count Portalis :

As regards myself, Monsieur le Comte, when you were good enough to allow me an additional sum of thirty thousand francs, you were under the impression that none of the cardinals would stay with me. Now, M. de Clermont-Tonnerre put up here with his suite, consisting of two Conclavists, an ecclesiastical secretary, a lay secretary, a valet, two manservants, and a French cook, beside a Roman groom of the chambers, a master of ceremonies, three footmen, a coachman, and all the Italian establishment which a cardinal is obliged to keep up here.

Truly, as Carlyle might have said, an expensive M. de Clermont-Tonnerre !

But the Archbishop of Toulouse was worse. This clumsy prelate had sprained his ankle getting out of his carriage after crossing the Arno, and, not being able to dine at Chateaubriand's table,

requires two or three courses at different hours, and horses and carriages for his guests and friends. My reverend visitor will certainly not pay his expenditure here ; he will go and leave his bills to me. I shall have to pay, not only the cook, the laundress, the livery stable keeper, etc., etc., but also the two surgeons who came to look at his lordship's leg, the shoemaker who makes his white and purple slippers, and the tailor who has " confectioned " the cloaks, cassocks, neckbands, and the whole outfit of the cardinal and the abbés.

To the poor exile in his garret in Holborn thirty thousand francs would have been a fortune beyond the dreams of avarice, but, with cardinals to feed, it was, as Chateaubriand proceeds to explain, a mere bagatelle. He does not seem, however, to have got any more, and left Rome heavily in debt.

In another, but not sincerer, vein he writes to Madame Récamier :

I have just left the Sistine Chapel, where I attended Tenebræ and heard the Misere sung. I remembered that you had talked to me of this ceremony, which touched me a hundred times as much because of that.

The daylight was failing ; the shadows crept slowly across the frescoes of the chapel, and one distinguished but a few bold strokes of Michael Angelo's brush. The candles, extinguished one by one in turns, sent forth from their stifled flames a slender white smoke, a very natural image of life, which Scripture compares to a little smoke. The cardinals were kneeling, the Pope prostrate before the same altar where a few days before I had seen his predecessor ; the admirable prayer of penance and mercy which succeeded the Lamentations of the Prophet rose at intervals in the silence of the night. The Catholic Heiress was there on her seven hills with all her memories ; but instead of the powerful pontiffs, those cardinals who contended for precedence with monarchs, a poor, old, paralysed Pope, without family or support, and princes of the Church, without splendour, announced the end of a power which has civilised the modern world. The masterpieces of the arts were disappearing with it, were fading away on the walls and ceilings of the Vatican, that half-abandoned palace. Inquisitive strangers separated from the Unity of the Church assisted at the ceremony on their way, and took the place of the Community of the Faithful.

Could Chateaubriand have lived to see the final departure of the fading remnants of the Pope's temporal power, his quick spirit would not have failed to perceive signs in the heavens of a renewed spiritual authority.

Chateaubriand greatly enjoyed his walks in Rome—a Rome in which, to the great joy of that Prince in Philistia, His Britannic Majesty's Roman Consul is no longer to be seen, "with her gardens full of ruins, with enclosures planted with trees and vines, with cloisters where rise palm trees and cypresses—the first resembling Eastern women, the second God-serving nuns." Nothing of the kind now meets the eye, which is regaled by quite other sights. Listen to His Majesty's Consul :

Suburbs have risen over the vineyards outside the city walls, old quarters have been superseded by large and commodious buildings. The Tiber is permanently embedded all along its urban course between two gigantic embankments, on which fine houses overlooking the river have been constructed ; solid granite bridges, meant to defy the ravages of time, have been thrown across the two embankments ; new and wide thoroughfares have been opened. In one word, the city has been completely modernised and rendered in all respects quite sanitary.

In Chateaubriand's Memoirs you can still wander through a Rome which, though without any of the attractions described so lovingly by the Consul, has held captive many hearts to whom hideous yellow flats, embankments, new thoroughfares, and granite bridges would appeal in vain.

Of Chateaubriand's visit to Charles X. in his exile in Bohemia, and his excellent and, of course, neglected advice as to the education of the young Henri Cinq, there is no time to tell.

If these Memoirs are not both readable and well worth reading, I should not know where to look for a book that was either the one thing or the other. The translator is entitled to the thanks of all good Englishmen who, despite French novels and the French play, cannot read the language of Chateaubriand without a dictionary.